The Compassionate and Commercially A[illegible] Care Manager

Edited by
Dr Richard Hawkins
Editor-in-Chief, *Caring Times*

The Compassionate and Commercially Aware Care Manager
First published in 2017

Hawker Publications, Culvert House, Culvert Road, London SW11 5DH
Tel 020 7720 2108. Website: www.careinfo.org

Acknowledgements

I am very grateful to the many people within the care home sector whose sustained belief that care management should be both compassionate and commercially aware has provided the inspiration and encouragement for this manual.

In particular I would like to thank Geoff Hodgson, Irene Johnson, Mozghan Shephazad, Nicola Jones and Wilsa John for their much appreciated in-house contributions. I would also like to thank Chris Manthorp, Emma Charlton, Phil Benson, the Hallmark Healthcare management team, Julia Clinton, Keith Lewin, Paul Birley, Andy Bradley and Tim Leeman for their valuable feedback and contributions.

British Library Cataloguing in Publication Data
A catalogue record of this book is available from the British Library

ISBN 9781874790242

Typesetting, design and editing by Prepare to Publish Ltd
mail@preparetopublish.com

Front cover design by Wheelhouse Design
info@wheelhouse.co.uk

Front cover illustration by Kieran Ingram
Printed by DG3, London

Hawker Publications publishes *Caring Times*, the *Journal of Dementia Care* and a selection of care and dementia books available for purchase on the website www.careinfo.org.

Dedication

My experience over 25 years is that most care managers are compassionate people who want the very best for their residents but are often not sufficiently commercially aware to be able to make the best use of their own potential and the resources available to them. This manual is therefore dedicated to people doing an incredibly challenging job – care managers and training care managers – in the hope that it can encourage and help them to be both compassionate and commercially aware so that they can provide the very best quality of care for the vulnerable people they are working with.

This manual is also dedicated to the best family in the world – to Jane, Rory, Lois and Kit – with the greatest affection and thanks.

Contents

Introduction

There is an Indian proverb (see Rumer Godden, *A House with Four Rooms*) which says that everyone is a house with four rooms: one mental, one physical, one emotional, and one spiritual. In *The Compassionate and Commercially Aware Care Manager* we are going to ask you to spend a lot of time in your mental room and also in your emotional room. A healthy, successful and complete manager, however, will visit the other rooms too every day – perhaps by necessity only for a short time – because the physical and spiritual sides to your life must not be ignored or neglected.

The key message behind this manual for the care home manager in the independent (private, charitable and not-for-profit) sector is that to be a truly successful, compassionate manager you also have to be a commercially aware manager.

Some people question whether it is possible to combine being both caring and financially successful but we at *Caring Times* argue that unless a care home is commercially successful it is very difficult, however compassionate and caring the manager is, for the care home to be a place where residents are truly happy, well cared for and live their lives to their full potential. By understanding the basics of business and commerce and how to make the best use of your financial resources you are putting yourself in the best possible position to provide the best possible quality of care for the vulnerable people you work with.

Care providers are often challenged whether they would pass the 'mum test' – the test which asks whether you are providing a compassionate care environment in which everyone would be happy for their mum to live. Would *your* mum be happy to live there? Our argument in this manual is that it is difficult to pass the mum test unless you are commercially aware so that you use your resources to benefit and help your residents to the maximum.

This manual tells you what you need to know about commercial awareness. It will fill gaps in your knowledge, explain commercial terminology which can sometimes be obscure and difficult, and give *you* the understanding and knowledge to help you make a real difference in your home and become a very successful manager – in every sense.

All sections start with questions about aspects of commercial awareness which will make you think again about your current knowledge and understanding. Try to answer these questions honestly in the spaces provided, without referring to the text which follows, because by doing so you will start the questioning and thinking which you need for your successful climb to becoming a great manager.

The text is designed for quick learning and reference – for example we often use checklists so that you can run through them and make sure you have not forgotten anything. Each section finishes with self-reflection – an opportunity for you to write down action points for yourself and for your care home based on the information you have learnt in the section and any personal reflection you may have had – we will want well informed, committed action!

Sounds interesting? Good, let's get started 😃.

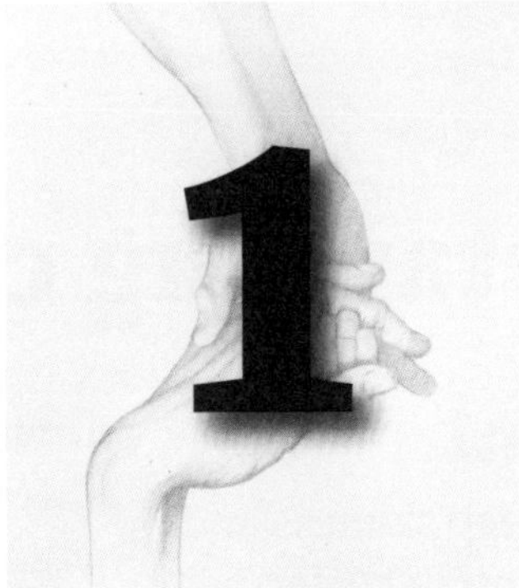

You as a Compassionate Manager

What is your understanding of compassion?

What do you think compassionate people have in common?

In Section 1 we will discuss:

- **Understanding more about compassion**
- **Becoming that wonderful person – a compassionate manager**

Understanding compassion

What is compassion?

Compassion is the feeling of deep sadness and sorrow for another person who is suffering, accompanied by a strong wish to help that person. It is this deep desire to help that makes being compassionate such a powerful force. It is quite different from showing sympathy which is a passive emotion and does not suggest any intention to help.

The great religions value compassion:

- **Allah** says that to be godly is to be compassionate. Those who wish to find Him will succeed only if they are kind and compassionate to the common people.
- **Buddha** states "loving kindness and compassion is all of our practice".
- One of the most famous parables in the **Christian Bible** tells the story of the compassion of an outsider, a Samaritan, for a man who has fallen sick by the roadside and who he helps when many others have walked by on the other side of the road.
- **The Dalai Lama** believes that individual acts of compassion by single people increase harmony for the whole world. He has said: "Love and compassion are necessities. They are not luxuries. Without them, humanity cannot survive."
- Compassion is the basis for ahimsa, a core virtue in **Hindu** philosophy.
- **Judaism** has 13 'attributes of compassion'.

Acts of compassion take place all over the world among many different people and in many different situations. It seems that humans have what researcher Dacher Keltner calls ''a compassionate instinct''. In other words compassion is a natural and automatic response which has helped humans to survive.

The naturalist and biologist Charles Darwin, who is said to have first used the words ''the survival of the fittest'' when describing those who do best in the natural world didn't actually say them at all (Herbert Spencer did). Darwin actually believed in 'survival of the kindest'. Indeed, in *The Descent of Man* and *Selection in Relation to Sex* (1871), Darwin makes a case for "the greater strength of the social or maternal instincts than that of any other instinct or motive".

If you want to be more attractive to potential mates - be kind. Both women and men agree that kindness/compassion is one of the most attractive traits and greatly valued.

Why are **the lives of compassionate people** like the saint and missionary Mother Teresa so inspiring? It seems that seeing someone else behaving in a loving and compassionate way raises our own mood and that this improvement helps to inspire us to help others also – setting up a chain reaction of goodwill.

Leaders and managers who are compassionate and self-sacrificing can also influence employees to be more compassionate. Indeed, compassion and acts of generosity can become catching. Happiness spreads and, because the people around us are happy, we in turn become happier. It has often been said that the act of giving appears to be as pleasurable as, if not more than, the act of receiving.

Recently there has been increasing pressure to put compassion at the heart of how health and social care is delivered. NHS Improvement, for example, has highlighted compassionate leadership as one of the five conditions it is seeking to create in its national framework *Developing people: improving care.*

https://improvement.nhs.uk/resources/developing-people-improving-care/

Joan Halifax

Roshi Joan Halifax is an American Zen Buddhist teacher, anthropologist, ecologist, civil rights activist, hospice caregiver and author. She is known for sitting at the bedside of terminally ill patients, and for creating a training programme, *Being With Dying*, for clinicians which addresses the compassionate care of people who are seriously ill and dying.

One of Joan's core messages is 'Strong back, soft front'. Speaking in her 2010 TED Talk, Joan said: "I want to address the issue of compassion. Compassion has many faces. Some of them are fierce; some of them are wrathful; some of them are tender; some of them are wise.

"I was so privileged to be able to teach in a hospice on the outskirts of Bangalore. And early in the morning, I went into the ward. In that hospice, there were 31 men and women who were actively dying. And I walked up to the bedside of an old woman who was breathing very rapidly, fragile, obviously in the latter phase of active dying. I looked into her face. I looked into the face of her son sitting next to her, and his face was just riven with grief and confusion.

"And I remembered a line from the Mahabharata, the great Indian epic: "What is the most wondrous thing in the world, Yudhisthira?" And Yudhisthira replied, "The most wondrous thing in the world is that all around us people can be dying and we don't realise it can happen to us." I looked up. Tending those 31 dying people were young women from villages around Bangalore. I looked into the face of one of these women, and I saw in her face the strength that arises when natural compassion is really present. I watched her hands as she bathed an old man...

"And when I worked in the prison system, it was so clear to me, this: that many of us in this room, and almost all of the men that I worked with on death row, the seeds of their own compassion had never been watered. That compassion is actually an inherent human quality. It is there within every human being. But the conditions for compassion to be activated, to be aroused, are particular conditions...

"And what is fascinating is that compassion has enemies, and those enemies are things like pity, moral outrage, fear. And you know, we have a society, a world that is paralysed by fear. And in that paralysis, of course, our capacity for compassion is also paralysed...

''Now we know from neuroscience that compassion has some very extraordinary qualities. For example: A person who is cultivating compassion, when they are in the presence of suffering, they feel that suffering a lot more than many other people do. However, they return to baseline a lot sooner. This is called resilience. Many of us think that compassion drains us, but I promise you it is something that truly enlivens us.

"You know, if compassion is so good for us, I have a question. Why don't we train our children in compassion? If compassion is so good for us, why don't we train our health care providers in compassion so that they can do what they're supposed to do, which is to really transform suffering?"

"

Many of us think that compassion drains us, but I promise you it is something that truly enlivens us

“

Compassion is the basis of all morality.
– Arthur Schopenhauer, German philosopher

The six Cs

The 2013 Francis Report into neglect and abuse at Mid Staffordshire Foundation Trust highlighted **the 6 Cs needed in the care sector**:

C

- Care
- Commitment
- Competence
- **Compassion**
- Communication
- Courage

Compassionate and inclusive leaders can deliver high-performing health systems based on a culture where their valued staff can deliver big quality and efficiency improvements quickly. Compassionate leaders achieve these successes by paying close attention to all their staff and trying hard to understand the situations they face. Then they take thoughtful and appropriate action to help.

Although being compassionate seems to come easier to some people than others, **everyone can be helped by some training**. Compassion and 'loving-kindness' meditation courses are available, often based on traditional Buddhist practices, which may help cultivate compassion (details are available on Amazon, Google and elsewhere). Cultivating compassion does not require years of study, and positive results and a greater understanding and practice can be achieved quite quickly.

The compassionate manager

A care manager wanting to help is therefore **that wonderful person – a compassionate manager**. However, a person who wants to help needs resources to transform their desire into real action. This is where this manual comes into play because **we recognise that the first instinct of most managers is to want to help, to make a difference to vulnerable people, to run compassionate homes which make residents happy**. But the challenge for such managers (and you are probably one of them) is how to achieve these ambitions with the resources you have been given, which in some cases may be quite limited. We make no apologies for saying that in order to achieve these ambitions you need to be commercially aware, and that by understanding commerce and business better you will be able to run a financially successful home which makes it possible for you to achieve your wider ambitions. This manual will help you to do that.

Story

An Indian family made up of father, mother and two teenage daughters came to live in the UK. They worked hard and in time had saved enough to be able to buy a small care home. It proved more difficult than they had expected to fill the home with residents. However, they had done their business plan carefully and it seemed they could survive. As they had empty beds, their relatives and friends and friends of friends started asking to stay, promising they would pay the fees but had short term cash problems. The owners figured that a promise of cash was better than none so they started to accept these residents. What they had not anticipated was the impact the increased staffing levels, food bills and utility costs had on their cash-flows. Before long they had to close. Sadly, lack of commercial awareness resulted in their kind hearts influencing their heads to make bad financial decisions which ruined a potentially good business that could have helped a lot of vulnerable people in the community over many years.

Self-directed reflection

Having read Section 1 about compassion, write below the five things you will do/change immediately

Notes

Commercial Awareness

What do you understand by the phrase 'commercial awareness'?

Why is it important for a care home manager to be commercially aware?

In Section 2 we will discuss:

- ➤ **Commercial awareness**
- ➤ **Business organisation**
- ➤ **Stakeholders**
- ➤ **Commercial analysis using the SWOT analysis tool**
- ➤ **Building a stronger business**

What is commercial awareness?

Introduction

Being commercially aware is understanding the broad basics of business and combining that knowledge with a deep understanding of your commercial role within your organisation and how to make a success of it.

For the purposes of this manual, that role is being a care home manager (or wanting/training to be one). The manager's role is vitally important because it is the foundation upon which the whole care home is built. It is a tough job, not least because it requires you to develop many different skills. Many people will depend on you and the main person you will depend on is... yourself, including your values, your personality, your truthfulness, your knowledge, your energy, your resilience... and yes, your compassion.

Being 'aware' requires you to continue throughout your working life to be interested in the commercial world around you – both inside your care home(s) and outside. If you keep that sense of wonder, that desire to learn and understand, to have an open mind for everything, you will be successful in your career and go on to manage lots of homes very well.

Commercial awareness is an attitude of mind. It's about being interested:

1. **In the big, wide business world out there**:
   - ☐ how it is set up and why?
   - ☐ what's changing?
   - ☐ what's new?
   - ☐ how customers are changing
   - ☐ what kind of businesses are going to be successful in the future.
2. **In the smaller business world you live in** (ie your care home and the organisation that owns it)
   - ☐ how does it work?
   - ☐ who funds it?
   - ☐ who matters?
   - ☐ how well does your care home fit into the organisation?
   - ☐ what opportunities might there be for you?
   - ☐ has your organisation got a future?
3. **In bringing the two worlds together** so you can make the best possible job of being a care manager.

Commercial awareness is also about having an understanding of:

- ☐ **Why what you do is helpful and valuable** to the residents, to the residents' families and friends, to your organisation and to the local community
- ☐ **Which service(s) is/are important** and deserving of your constant focus
- ☐ **Which people find your service(s) valuable** (your clients) and therefore deserving of your constant focus
- ☐ **What your clients are willing to pay** for your service(s)
- ☐ **How successful** your care home and organisation is
- ☐ **What your commercial competitors are offering** and what new services they might be setting up
- ☐ **Whether there are other, new commercial services** which you might develop
- ☐ How likely your clients are to **recommend your service(s).**

Commercial awareness and strategic planning

Equipped with the right attitude of mind and the appropriate understanding, the next stage is coming up with a **strategic plan:**

- **A strategy is driven by a vision**. NASA, the American Space Programme, had a vision to put a man on the moon by the end of the 1960s. They succeeded in 1969. Your vision could be a bit simpler – to start with anyway – to become the best care home in your community.
- You will achieve your vision by having a

The 7-S Framework

- ☐ structure
- ☐ style
- ☐ staff
- ☐ strategy
- ☐ systems
- ☐ skills
- ☐ shared values

mission which is often described as the route map to achieving your vision. Many organisations have mission statements which they display prominently as reminders to clients and staff of their vision.

- The mission is guided by the **corporate culture** – what has been described by the famous management consultancy McKinsey as 'the way we do things round here'. They have helpfully pinpointed the seven factors which make organisations different as the **7-S Framework** (see left).

Risk

Being able to successfully judge the balance of risk versus benefit is very much part of becoming commercially aware. The nature of social care means there is an unavoidable variation in the levels of demand for care and consequently significant levels of risk for both providers (of care) and commissioners.

A sustainable market is more likely to be achieved where there is a fair balance of risk between commissioner and provider. For example, in block contracting the local authority takes the risk of funding empty beds while providers take the risk of turning away customers who may have been willing to pay higher fees. In spot contracting the provider retains the flexibility to sell all their beds – but risks not having a guaranteed income stream, while commissioners lack the comfort of having guaranteed beds.

Providers expect commissioners to take account of how their viability can be adversely affected if they shoulder a disproportionate amount of the risk. Equally, it is reasonable for commissioners to expect providers to recognise that if the local authority takes on too much risk they are likely to find themselves in a position which is neither affordable nor justifiable to taxpayers.

Taken from *Working with care providers to understand costs (2017)* CIPFA, DH, LGA, CPA and ADASS.

Business organisation

Let's now explain some of the broad basics of business:

1. **Understanding the different types of business organisation.**
2. **Understanding stakeholders and how they can work for you – not against you.**
3. **Understanding basic ideas on how to make a business successful.**

Types of business organisation

A business is an organisation which provides:

- **Goods**; in which case it is described as being in the manufacturing (or distribution/retailing) sector.
- Or **services** for its customers, in which case it is described as being in the service sector. Care homes provide a service so they are in the service sector.

Organisations can be classified by sector and by ownership:

- **Public sector** organisations are wholly or partly state owned eg the NHS.
- **Private sector** organisations are owned by individuals (or groups of them) eg Waitrose.
- **Voluntary sector** organisations which are not owned by anyone but are governed by trustees. These are usually charities and are designed to be not for profit, eg the Red Cross. This sector is also known as the *Third Sector*.

List five differing types of business/organisation you know and who owns them

Now think of your care home: what sector does it operate in and who owns it?

Types of businesses classified by ownership

Unincorporated businesses: If you start a business like being a plumber or electrician on your own, you are known as a **sole trader**. If you join with one or more people you become a **partnership** splitting the profit between the partners. The major problem with these types of businesses (and why so few care homes are organised like this) is that the people who run them are personally responsible for any debt the business may incur. If the business goes bust, the individuals will have to pay back the debt and if they do not have enough money to do so they will become bankrupt. This is called **unlimited liability** and it can make the sole traders or partners – as well as the people who are owed money by them – sleep very uneasily at night.

Incorporated businesses: An individual or individuals who do not wish to be personally liable for business debts can **incorporate** (ie register their business at Companies House) and form a **limited company**.

A limited company (Ltd) is an organisation that runs a business – it's responsible in its own right for everything it does and its finances are separate from its owners' personal finances.

A company can be owned by one or more people known as **shareholders** and is run by one or more **directors** forming a **Board of Directors**. Shareholders do not necessarily have to be directors and directors do not necessarily have to be shareholders. This separation can be a good thing because it encourages the directors to be innovative, but it can also be a bad thing because it may encourage directors who are not shareholders to take too much risk.

The company can keep any profit it makes though it will have to pay corporation tax on it. After tax is paid the company can then either:

- Share out the money (as **dividends**) to its shareholders in proportion to how many shares they each own.
- Or keep the profit (as **retained profit)** ready for hard times or to use as an investment to grow the company.
- Or **do a bit of both** the above.

Limited liability partnership (LLP) is a relatively new (2001) type of incorporated business model which you should know about because you will meet them in your business life. It is not used as a business model to run care homes. An LLP is like a limited company (for example it has to be registered with Companies House and report to HM Revenue and Customs) but also has some of the features of a partnership. This mix makes it attractive to people such as accountants, law firms, dentists and designers who, as members, appreciate being able to manage their organisation flexibly and have the tax benefits and distribution of profits of a general partnership structure but, at the same time, also benefit from the advantage of the reduced financial liabilities of a limited company. So, unlike with partnerships, members' financial responsibility is limited to the capital they have invested or any financial commitment they may have made to their LLP. Financial and legal responsibilities, therefore, stay with the LLP not with the members.

There are also several types of limited companies:

- **Private company limited by shares**: Most small to medium sized companies (SMEs) in the UK take this form. The company issues shares which shareholders buy. The money collected is known as **share capital**. If the company runs into financial difficulties and has to be closed each shareholder is not at risk of having to pay for any company debts. (What they paid for their shares is the limit of their liability.)

Saint Teresa

Manfredo Ferrari

Saint (Mother) Teresa is known for her life's work with poor and dying people. She was awarded the Nobel Peace Prize in 1979 in recognition of her work "in bringing help to suffering humanity" and canonised as a saint in 2016 by Pope Francis who said "Mother Teresa, in all aspects of her life, was a generous dispenser of divine mercy, making herself available for everyone through her welcome and defence of human life, those unborn and those abandoned and discarded".

The order Missionaries of Charity was founded by Saint Teresa in 1950. Throughout the 1950s and 60s, the order opened a leper colony, an orphanage, a nursing home, a family clinic and several mobile health clinics.

"Be happy in the moment, that's enough. Each moment is all we need, not more." – Saint Teresa

> *Compassion is sometimes the fatal capacity for feeling what it is like to live inside somebody else's skin. It is the knowledge that there can never really be any peace and joy for me until there is peace and joy finally for you too.*
> *– Frederick Buechner, American clergyman*

- **Private company limited by guarantee:** These companies have members (not shareholders) who act as guarantors by financially backing the organisation up to a specific amount. If things go wrong, the only liability members have is for the amount they guaranteed to the company. This type of structure is commonly favoured by charities, voluntary groups, and other non-profit organisations.
- **Public limited companies:** When private companies are successful they may decide that the only way to raise the money they need to become even more successful is to raise it from the public. They join a stock market, for example, the London Stock Exchange or the Alternative Investment Market (AIM) by means of a **listing** or **flotation** and become a public limited company (PLC). Their shares are now listed on the stock exchange which means that the public can buy and sell them – hence the slightly confusing term 'public'.

Charities and not-for-profit organisations

Because care homes are designed to help vulnerable people they are often owned and run by charities. These types of care homes are frequently described as being in **the third sector** (ie not state or privately owned) or as being in the **voluntary sector** (because some of the work may be done by volunteers). Increasing financial and regulatory demands have required them to be run much like private companies with a chief executive and a board of trustees/directors. **Charities are not designed to make a profit but they do aim to make a surplus** (the difference between their income and their expenses). It is important they make a surplus so that they can reinvest in their homes to maintain them at the very best standard.

State/council-owned homes

We expect to receive certain benefits from the State such as police and firemen to protect us, water, roads and pavements, healthcare and education paid for by our taxes. In the past many vulnerable people such as elderly people, or those with a learning disability, were cared for by the State in council-run care homes. However more recently many councils have decided that financial and regulatory pressures mean that they can spend their budgets more effectively by placing the people they are funding in private and charity care homes rather than in their own. So the number of council owned and run care homes has declined significantly to less than 5% of all care homes.

Stakeholders

Interested people

A care home has many people interested in its operations both internally within the home and outside. These interested people are known as **stakeholders** and they are likely to have different views and interests which, if not managed properly, can cause conflict, and result in damage to the care home. Good examples of such conflict are management fighting with staff over their wages, or suppliers fighting with management over the cost of their goods and services.

The impact various stakeholders can have on a business's operations is beginning to be acknowledged in what is known as **stakeholder theory**. This theory recognises the importance of stakeholders, gives guidelines on working with them and also goes a step further by suggesting that every organisation has a responsibility and ethical duty towards them in its operations (see box overleaf).

Stakeholder theory says organisations have a responsibility to behave well towards clients, suppliers, staff and the local community and, in order to succeed over a long time, executives of an organisation must work hard to keep the interests of all its stakeholders going in the same direction.
So, innovation to keep stakeholders working together is much more important than the easy strategy of encouraging stakeholders to battle against each other and then perhaps benefit from the short-term fall-out. Instead, by working with all stakeholders rather than against them, executives will create a fantastic organisation (eg a care home) which benefits everyone.

Which stakeholders matter to you most?

As a compassionate and commercially aware care manager you will know that your most important stakeholders are your residents. But life is not as simple as that – you also need to work out who the most influential stakeholders are who are going to help you make your home the best it can possibly be, and/or help any projects or ideas you wish to pursue. This process is called **stakeholder analysis** and you should do it all the time to improve the quality of care you provide for your residents, to help you become a better manager and improve the quality of your project planning.

Stakeholder analysis helps you to learn who the key people are that you will need to win over and work with. **It involves four steps**:

1. **Identify your key stakeholders**: Have a brainstorming session and write down all the people who are involved in the running of your home and all those who could be affected by a special project. Include everyone, thinking most carefully about those who support you and those who are most likely not to.

2. **Prioritise those who are most likely to be influential:** From the list you have generated in your brainstorming session use the power interest grid below to map them into their relevant categories. This will show you what level of communication you need with each of them:

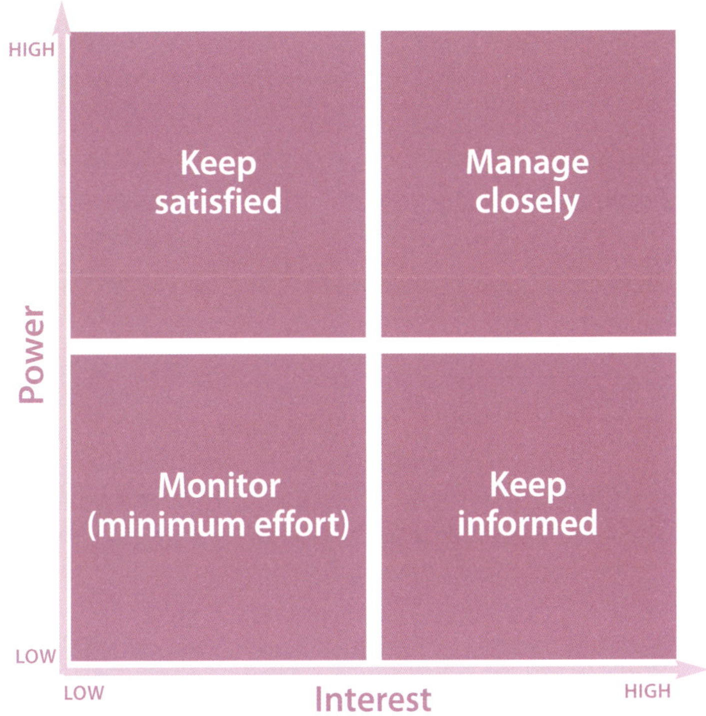

Power Interest Grid

- Those people that fall in the **high power and high interest section** of the grid are key to your work and/or project. You need to work with them very closely. You must keep them fully engaged at all times and make the greatest effort to satisfy their interests, especially those who may oppose you. There is a saying 'keep your friends close but your enemies even closer' which is probably a bit over-dramatic for the care home scenario but is good advice.
- Those in **the high power but less interest** category need to be kept up to date but do not overwhelm them with so much information that they become bored with your message.

The responsibility of organisations (like care homes) to stakeholders:

Stakeholders	Organisations' responsibilities
To owners/shareholders	To maximise shareholder value eg by growing the company and giving them good dividends
To employees	To provide salaries and benefits and a safe, satisfying working environment. To make sure employees have the skills and knowledge to do their job well
To residents/clients/customers	To deliver high quality care, products and services
To suppliers	To honour contracts and pay them on time
To the community	To safeguard the environment, care compassionately for vulnerable people, and be an important community asset including providing local work
To the government	To pay taxes and obey company and employment law
To regulators	To follow industry rules and codes of practice and make sure care homes are safe places to live in and work
To banks and financial institutions	To service debt responsibly and repay all money lent as contractually agreed

- Those in the **low power, high interest** category are people you need to keep informed. Communicate with them to ensure that they have no major problems. These people can often be very helpful with the detail of your project.
- Those in the **low power, low interest** group need to be monitored and informed but not bored with excessive communication.

3. **Build a wide networks of contacts**. Successful managers network all the time so they have a wide pool of supporters to support them improving their home, for a new project (or dare we say it? – for a promotion).

> *Love and compassion are necessities, not luxuries. Without them, humanity cannot survive.*
> *– 14th Dalai Lama*

4. Once you have identified who the stakeholders in your project are and what action you are going to take with each of them, your next task is to **put your plans into action**, taking into account your stakeholders' likely reactions and how you are going to work with them best. By doing so you will improve the quality of your planning and budgeting and be much more likely to get stakeholder support, reduce opposition and be successful. Hopefully, stakeholders' views are rational but they may also be emotional and unfounded so think ahead and be ready.

Think of a project (it can be internal or external) you want to embark on in your care home. Use stakeholder analysis to find out who your key stakeholders are and lay out a plan of how you are going to get their support.

Building a stronger business

There are four foundations for making a business better. They build on one another:

1. **Right clients.** You need to find the right clients – those who want your product/service and have the money to pay for them.

+

2. **Excellent client/customer care.** Your total focus should be on serving your clients better. If you get what is often described as 'client/customer care' right you are moving a long way towards making your whole organisation successful. It is too easy when there is so much bureaucracy to deal with, to take your eye off the ball and neglect your lifeblood – your residents. The less mistakes you make and the less time and money you waste putting those mistakes right, the better you serve your clients.

+

3. **Care is a people business.** You should understand and treat your clients and staff as people. By treating people with care and compassion you are showing that you value them which is exactly what every person wants.

+

4. **Controlling costs.** By understanding and transforming your costs you can afford to improve the quality of life of your clients.

=

Profit and reinvestment: the cycle of hope

If you find the right clients, provide brilliant customer care, treat your clients and staff well and control your costs **you are likely to make a profit.** With this profit you can reinvest time and money in your home – its structure, fabric, stakeholders, staff and training – so it remains a place of quality and renewal. And continues to make a profit **so that the successful cycle of hope can continue.**

The SWOT commercial analysis tool

There are a number of tools and processes that you can use to analyse your care home's commercial position in the care home market place.

We will examine the most useful and popular tool (SWOT Analysis) in detail in this chapter.

In the EXTRA INFO section at the back of the manual we will examine two other tools which are widely used also to analyse organisations:

- PESTLE analysis examines the external factors which may impact on your organisation/care home.
- Porter's 5 Forces helps you analyse your competitive position.

All these tools have been successful because they are generally easy to understand and to use. Don't be put off by the letters.

SWOT analysis

SWOT analysis is the most commonly used tool because it is so easy and flexible. You may then decide that you want to use the other tools too.

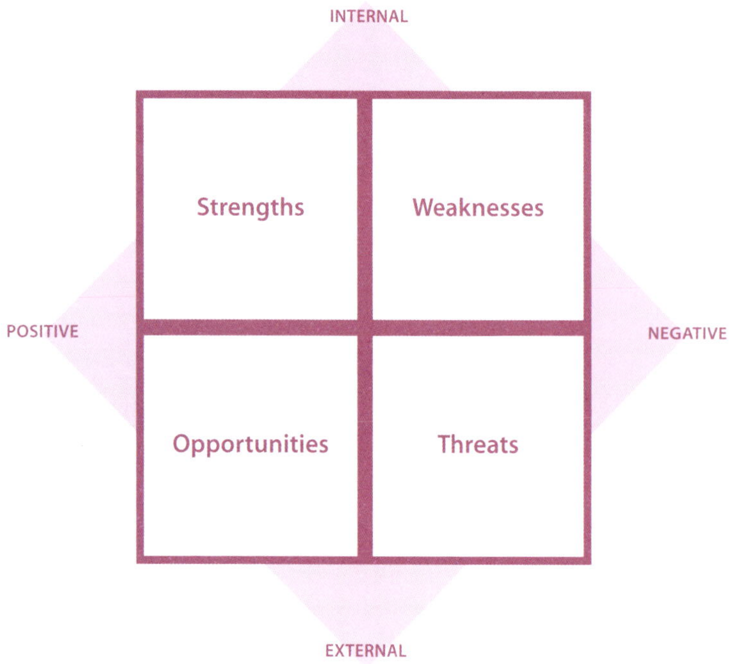

SWOT stands for

Strengths: by which is meant all the positive things your organisation is good at and which give it an advantage over other organisations eg a very well trained, enthusiastic staff.

Weaknesses: by which is meant all the things your organisation does badly and which will have a negative effect on your organisation achieving its objectives eg old, inefficient admin systems which are outdated and need updating.

Opportunities: by which is meant the exciting developments taking place in and around your organisation that it could take advantage of – big and small - to make a difference in achieving or exceeding its objectives.

Threats: by which is meant developments, internal and external, taking place in the environment around your organisation which could damage it.

SWOT is a very flexible tool and can be applied at many different levels.

A SWOT analysis helps you understand your business better so that you can make better strategic decisions about how to move it forward. It considers:

- The strengths and weaknesses within your organisation (internal) allowing you to make changes based on facts and logic.
- Opportunities and threats externally. Having decided what your strengths and weaknesses internally are you can decide how best to adapt to – and take advantage of – changes in the external environment.

Suggestions about how to carry out SWOT analysis:

1. Analyse your organisation **internally**. Write down its strengths and weaknesses in terms of the following factors:

- ☐ **Strategy**: is your care home moving in the right direction now? Is the performance matching the mission statement and company objectives? Do you have an updated, strategic plan in place?
- ☐ **Culture and structure**: are you satisfied with the home's focus on their clients /customers? Is the team motivated to be the best?
- ☐ **Brand and reputation**: are you satisfied with your reputation in your local community and with your local commissioners? Is there more that you could do?
- ☐ **Staff**: are your staff happy and well trained? Do you have less staff turnover than other homes? Are the staff fully client focused?
- ☐ **Money:** do you have records of exactly what each of your residents is paying? Are your costs tightly controlled? Do you have cash flow problems?
- ☐ **Resources**: is your home in good physical shape? If you have a garden, is it well looked after? Does your IT do what you need from it and is it up-to-date and reliable?

2. Analyse your organisation **externally**. Write down its opportunities and threats in terms of the following factors:
   - ☐ **Marketplace:** are you up to date with the care home market nationally and locally? Is there a chance for mergers and acquisitions or do you run a risk of being taken over?
   - ☐ **Competition:** have you done some secret shopping to see what other care homes are offering locally and whether they represent a threat to you, or whether you could learn from them about additional opportunities?
   - ☐ **Recruitment:** what are local care homes and businesses offering in terms of pay and benefits? Could they poach your staff or could you come up with your own staff package which is very attractive to the competition?
   - ☐ **Marketing:** how good is your marketing? Could it be better? If so, how?
   - ☐ **Market share:** what percentage of the care market are you serving? Are you nearly full? Are you getting lots of enquiries for your beds? Are leads recorded and followed up?
   - ☐ **Other external factors** that might affect your home eg the local authority has just announced a 4% increase in the fees it will pay to care homes (opportunity), or a big homecare organisation has just bought the small local homecare company (threat).

3. **Action plan.** Having done your analysis it is now time to take action, for example by following the suggestions below:
   - ☐ **Using strengths** eg using your current profitability to increase your staff training budget to reduce even further your staff turnover.
   - ☐ **Minimising weaknesses** eg offering your staff subsidised public travel so that reaching your lovely but remote location in the country is less of a problem for them.
   - ☐ **Taking opportunities** eg opening the wing of the home you had to close two years ago now that local authority fees have gone up 4%.
   - ☐ **Warding off threats** eg offering your largely unused lounge free to local clubs to counter the perception that care homes are prisons where old people go to die.

Learn from meerkats

Behave like a meerkat on look-out. They focus on two jobs. One is to spot any threats and warn their communities. The other is to look out for opportunities – they can't make body fat so they have to find fresh food to eat every day. That focuses their minds!

Conclusion: If you focus on spotting threats and finding opportunities you won't go far wrong.

Charles J Sharp

Self–directed reflection

Write down five important points from Section 2 which are going to make a difference to how you work:

How Care Homes are Funded

What do you think are the two most common ways of funding care homes?

Care homes are funded in all sorts of different ways. A combination of bank debt and money from the owners and others (equity) is probably the most common way. In Section 3 we will help you learn more about:

- Banks and debt
- Bonds
- Grants
- Other sources: hire/lease purchase, factoring, business angels, crowdfunding
- Equity
- Family and friends
- Leasing

Banks and debt

Banks are often the main way (sometimes helped by **equity backers** – see below) a private care home business is funded. The two options are:

- **Long-term loans:** These can be taken for a number of years and can be provided either at a variable interest rate based on the **bank rate** or at a fixed rate for an agreed number of years. Fixed rates tend to be higher initially because there is more risk for the bank but are considered to be safer for businesses because they know exactly how much they will have to pay every month and this cannot be raised until the **term** of the loan finishes.

  In theory the loan should be paid back to the bank when the term is completed but, unless the business has been incredibly successful or sold, the loan is usually rolled over with a new interest rate and term.

- **Short-term lending:** These loans are provided by banks in the form of **overdrafts.** Overdrafts are funds provided by the bank to help an organisation when it needs cash to pay suppliers and staff, for example, and it does not have enough at that particular moment but will do when it has collected its own debts. They are usually easier to arrange and change than long-term loans; but they are more expensive than loans, and are instantly repayable to the bank on demand if the bank is worried about what is happening to the organisation and wants to get as much loaned money back as quickly as possible. Despite these disadvantages a little over a quarter of businesses use overdrafts as core funding.

Equity

Equity is money invested in a company by people who believe the company has a future and will reward them financially in return for their investment. Each person who invests (**shareholder**) gets **shares** (also called **stock**) in direct proportion to how much they have invested. So, if five people set up a company and each invests £200 the total **risk capital** invested is £1000 and each shareholder will own 20% of the company. They might decide that each share is worth £1, so each shareholder receives 200 £1 shares.

In time, if the company does well, the shares might become worth more than £1 each and the **shareholder** can make a **profit** by selling them at this higher price. Unfortunately quite a lot of start-ups tend to do badly rather than well in which case the value of the shares will go down and the investor will make a **loss**.

It is very important that you understand that equity is not a loan to the company so it will never be repaid. The only way shareholders get their equity back is by selling their shares. They can decide to do so at any time provided they can find somebody to buy them.

In the 18th century, when lots of new companies were starting up investors decided that they needed somewhere where they could gather and buy and sell shares (exchange them). So, **stock exchanges** were set up where **public companies'** (see page 22) shares were bought and sold. These (usually larger) companies were called 'public' because the public could buy/sell their shares.

Companies (usually smaller) whose shares cannot be bought/sold by the public are called **private companies** and their shares are not traded on a stock exchange. Shareholders in private companies can sometimes find it difficult to find an investor willing to pay the price they want which is one of these companies' main disadvantages.

There are, however, some companies which will invest cash in these private companies – they are known as private equity firms. These investments are often from institutions like funds and in return for the money they buy part of that company, receiving shares in return. They frequently take an active, expert part in the management of the company with a director on the board of directors and the money is used for growth, for example buying another company or for other specific investment strategies.

The purpose (**exit strategy**) of these private equity firms is to grow the company they have invested in using the cash they have provided to such a point their investments are worth a lot more money and then they can exit usually in one of two ways:

> *"Our human compassion binds us the one to the other - not in pity or patronizingly, but as human beings who have learnt how to turn our common suffering into hope for the future."*
> ***– Nelson Mandela, anti-apartheid politician, philanthropist and first black President of South Africa***

1. **The company is sold** for either cash or valuable shares in another company.
2. An **initial public offering** (**IPO**): shares of the company are offered to the public, and the money from the sale of their shares gives the private equity firm an excellent profit as well as a public market into which it can later sell any shares it has held on to.

Bonds

When companies (usually large ones with good reputations) need to **raise money,** for example for a new project like building care homes, one way to do it is to issue **bonds**. A bond works like a loan between an investor and a company. The investor agrees to give the company a specific amount of money for a specific period of time (say 10 or 20 years) at the end of which the money has to be repaid. In exchange investors receive interest payments at time intervals agreed in advance.

Since borrowing from a bank is perhaps the approach that comes most readily to mind for companies needing money, inevitably the question will be asked: "Why would a company issue bonds instead of just borrowing from a bank?" The answer is that the interest rate a company has to pay bond investors (holders) is often less than the interest rate they would be required to pay a bank to get a loan. So that's good for cashflow and profit.

Issuing bonds also gives a company much greater freedom to operate as they want, free from the restrictions that are often attached to bank loans. For example, a bank might insist (as part of its terms and conditions) on its loan being repaid in full before the company bought another company – something a bond holder would not be able to do.

Government bonds

In case you were wondering… because you have heard about them… but were too shy to ask… yes, governments also issue bonds known unsurprisingly as government bonds. These bonds (also known as gilts in the UK) are issued to raise money for the government to pay for special projects or everyday expenditure or help pay the interest on government debt. The first ever bond issued by a national government was issued by the Bank of England in 1694 to raise money to fund a war against France.

Salmaan Sana

Salmaan Sana is a consultant and facilitator who founded the non-profit organisation Compassion for Care which brings healthcare professionals and patients together for a common purpose – which is to create a more compassionate healthcare system. He is one of the creators of The Healthcare Leadership School, an international platform for personal leadership of students from all aspects of the healthcare system – future doctors, social workers, public health workers and nurses, medical students and other professionals in healthcare.

Applying for funding

When looking for funding for any new business or project, ensure your application looks good, is well researched and is succinct and truthful. Here are five suggestions to help you:

1. Be clear how much money you need

You need to be clear exactly how much money you need. It could be you want it to manage cash flow, install a lift, expand your care home or invest in more staff. Using this information you can work out exactly how much you'll need which will make it a lot easier for everyone to make informed decisions. Decide, from the start, exactly how you are going to raise the money you need. The clarity of your approach will show you are committed and know what you're doing, making your success more likely.

2. Write a clear business plan (see p33)

A carefully thought-out and well considered business plan for both the short and long term will show both your passion and ability. Lenders will be examining the finer details and will appreciate it being laid out in a readable and chronological way, outlining where the business is going, your future strategy and realistic financial forecasts.

3. Think again about your current funders

If you already have had or currently operate with a funder like a bank, think carefully how successful the relationship has been. This evaluation will give you a good indication of what you do and don't want from your next provider. The lending market has changed significantly recently – which is both a blessing and a curse. The variety offers a range of options to suit all needs, however it's also a lot harder to make your mind up who to go with. But making the right decision is really important – and so spending plenty of time doing the research is time well spent.

4. Do the right research to find the right funder

Knowing your market and your funding requirements is hugely worthwhile. Most people think first about bank funding and this remains the best funding for most people. However it is worth finding out about alternative sources such as asset finance, factoring and peer-to-peer (P2P) lending which may give your business/project a bit more breathing space and the chance to raise the money a little cheaper.

5. Get experienced and independent help

Sometimes working with an independent and experienced broker can relieve the chore of gathering data and having to make comparisons, allowing you to concentrate on starting/running your business while the broker researches and introduces you to a range of appropriate lenders with competitive rates. Some brokers try to 'blind you with science' so make sure you understand each stage of any proposal they may make. There is no shame in saying you don't understand something – after all, you are an expert in caring not finance. If they continue to try to pull the wool over your eyes the sooner you find yourself a new broker the better.

Family and friends

If a person needs money to start a business or keep a business going or finance a new project often the first people they think of are family and friends. There is mutual confidence and trust and it is an arrangement which has worked well on many, many occasions over hundreds of years.

Whether the money is borrowed or invested in shares, the key to success with family and friends is to make sure everything is written down, done legally and everybody knows exactly what the expectations are from them including the risks and rewards.

Everyone must understand that if there are business problems they will put a strain on family and friends' relationships and if the problems cannot be solved these relationships might finish... nastily (see Story, p32).

Grants

Consider the possibility of applying for grants, particularly for smaller projects which have a wide, community purpose and appeal. **Government and council grants** are available (although you will have to complete a lot of paperwork). **The other valuable source is charities**, some of which have a grant-giving ability designed to help develop services which fit their requirements and profile. It is sometimes worth applying to **large organisations like banks or companies** which give grants, but usually it is the **smaller, local charity** with whom your organisation may have personal links which proves more productive. Research and persistence will bring their reward. Good luck!

Leasing

If cash is in short supply, it may be worth using an **asset-financing technique** such as **leasing** equipment like expensive beds, specialist bathing equipment, hoists, vans, computers and office equipment rather than buying them outright.

The advantages of leasing are:

- You can use your valuable cash for more immediate needs like paying for gas, electricity and water or staff.
- You get the full use of the equipment without having to pay for their full cost immediately.
- You do not need a deposit.
- You know from the start exactly how much you are going to be paying – no nasty surprises!
- You can pay a bit more and get maintenance and emergency repairs included which is helpful on a Sunday evening when you have got better things to do than grubbing around underneath the dishwasher wondering why it is leaking.
- If the equipment can't be repaired you can usually get it replaced without cost (but check your lease's terms and conditions before signing them that free replacement is included).

The disadvantages of leasing are:

Leasing is almost always more expensive than buying outright. Sorry, in life you usually don't get something for nothing! So, when your equipment goes back to the owner at the end of the lease you will have paid more for it than if you had bought it outright. Before signing the lease, you need to check the terms and conditions very carefully so that you know exactly how much more expensive the proposed leasing is going to be. If it seems too expensive you can always try some negotiating – nothing to be lost by trying – or going somewhere else.

Story

After working for ten years as a care home manager Jean decided that she wanted to run her own home. She hadn't been able to save much herself so she needed help to find enough money to buy a home. Her widowed aunt thought the answer was to sell her big family home, give her niece enough money to get her started and go to Greece where she had always wanted to live. A 21-bed care home was bought and all went well until the letter from Greece arrived. In it Jean's aunt explained that she had just got remarried and she needed the money she had lent Jean so that the couple could buy a house in Athens. Jean was devastated. She was quite certain that her aunt had given her the money to buy her care home, not lent it to her. But there was no paperwork and the legal advice Jean received was that the money was her aunt's unless Jean could prove that she had been given it – which she couldn't. Her bank sadly explained that they couldn't lend her replacement funding because the home was not sufficiently profitable to be able to afford the large interest payments that would have to be paid. Jean lost everything – just because she didn't have a legal document which would have taken a lawyer half an hour to prepare plus two signatures.

Other funding options

Hire/lease purchase

Hire purchase, sometimes known as lease purchase, is different from leasing because you end up owning the equipment. You will usually be required to make a deposit (eg up to 40% of the equipment value) and then pay regular instalments until the hire purchase agreement finishes, say after three years, at which point you will own the equipment after a final payment. The option of owning the equipment after making all the required payments is attractive, particularly for equipment which you know lasts a long time. But guess what? Yes, you've got it – you pay even more than for leasing because you end up owning the equipment. But the huge difference is that you now have equipment which you can operate free of charge until it collapses or is no longer safe. Remember to set up new maintenance and repair contracts as they are likely to end when the hire purchase agreement ends.

Factoring

Getting people who owe money (debtors) to pay their bills is becoming harder and harder every year. Some (like councils) can take 60 to 90 days to pay which puts a great strain on cashflow. Some care homes find it helpful to avoid this cashflow strain by passing their debtors on to specialist (factoring) institutions which buy from them some or all of the money owed to the care home. These specialists pay the full amount immediately to the care home as cash after deducting a fee which can vary between 0.5 to 3.5 per cent of the total debt passed from the care home to them. These specialists then collect the full amount of money now owed to them, thus making a profit.

Business angels

Another possible funding source is people with funds (business angels) who wish to invest their money in either sectors they know well, or in exciting start-ups, or in organisations with a business plan they like. In return for their investment most business angels want more involvement than simply signing cheques made out to you! Some bring great experience and expertise and may have really valuable contacts.

Crowdfunding

Until recently, financing a business, project or venture involved asking a few people (like bankers) for large sums of money. Crowdfunding switches this idea around, using the internet to talk to thousands – if not millions – of potential funders, asking each of them to invest only a small amount of money. Typically, those seeking funds will set up a profile of their project on a website. They can then use social media, alongside traditional networks of friends, family and work acquaintances, to raise money. There are three different types of crowdfunding: donation, debt and equity.

1. Donation/reward crowdfunding
With this people invest simply because they believe in the cause and are not looking to make money. Donors have a social or personal motivation for putting their money in and expect nothing back, except perhaps to feel good about helping the project. Several care homes have raised funds for projects this way.

2. Debt crowdfunding
Investors receive their money back with interest. Also called peer-to-peer (P2P) lending, it enables money to be lent from person to person without the need for banks. Returns are financial, but investors also benefit from having contributed to the success of an idea they believe in.

3. Equity crowdfunding
This form of crowdfunding offers people the opportunity to invest (usually small amounts of) money (equity) in exchange for shares, or a small stake in the business, project or venture. These crowdfunded shares behave in every respect like regular shares. Their value can go up if the business, project or venture is successful or go down if it is not.

Writing a business plan

What is a business plan?
A business plan is a written document that describes your business. Think clearly who your audience is exactly and aim the information at them – no waffle!

Why you need a business plan
You'll need a business plan if you want to secure investment or a loan from a bank or other investor. It can also help to convince customers, suppliers and potential employees to support you.

What should a business plan include?
A business plan should include:
- ☐ brief summary of proposals and objective
- ☐ strategies and operations plan
- ☐ sales and marketing
- ☐ details of planned products and/or services
- ☐ analysis of competition
- ☐ management team and
- ☐ financial forecasts.

A business plan helps you to:
- clarify your business idea.
- spot potential problems.
- set out your goals simply and clearly.
- show potential investors what your plans. are and encourage them to invest.
- measure your progress.

Useful business plan websites
- Get good general advice on https://www.gov.uk/write-business-plan
- Download a free business plan template on The Prince's Trust website: www.princes-trust.org.uk/help-for-young-people/tools-resources/business-tools/business-plans
- You can also download a free cash flow forecast template (www.startuploans.co.uk/cash-flow-forecast-template/) or a business plan template (www.startuploans.co.uk/business-plan-template/) on the Start Up Loans website.
- Access example business plans on the Bplans website: www.bplans.co.uk
- Get detailed information about how to write a business plan on the Start Up Donut website: www.startupdonut.co.uk/business-planning/write-a-business-plan/writing-a-business-plan
- Read about the finance options available for businesses on the Business Finance Guide website: www.thebusinessfinanceguide.co.uk

Self-directed reflection

Using the information above and any additional ideas you might have, write down:

How you would fund a new care home?

How you would fund a new 12-bed extension plus communal rooms?

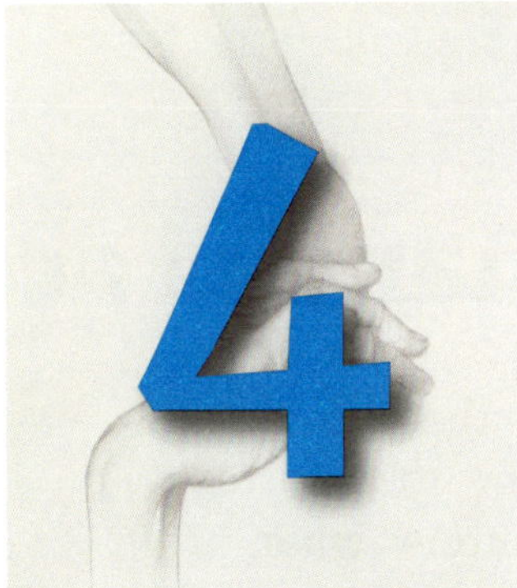

Understanding financial statements

What financial statements are you familiar with?

Why are financial statements needed? Write below as many reasons as you can think of.

In Section 4 we will discuss:

- **The structure for reporting financial accounts**
- **The structure of the profit and loss account**
- **The structure of the balance sheet**
- **The accounting year**
- **VAT**

Financial accounts

The financial reporting system that is in place today in the UK started in the 19th century during the Industrial Revolution when it became apparent that a mechanism was needed for people to:

- **Have access to enough financial information** to be able to make informed decisions about businesses. This information should include at least three **financial statements**:
  1. Profit and loss account (also known as the income statement).
  2. Balance sheet.
  3. Cashflow statement.
- **Be able to understand how businesses/organisations are performing** so potential investors could decide whether to invest in them.
- **Be able to start up or invest in businesses** while at the same time limiting their liability/responsibility if the business was to fail, leaving debts.

The profit and loss (P&L) account

The P&L account records an organisation's income and expenses over a fixed time (usually a month, a quarter or a year) and whether it has made a bottom-line profit or loss.

There's an accounting tradition that the figures for a loss are put in brackets – for example a £10,000 loss would be written as (10,000).

Bigger organisations with lots of zeros in the columns of their accounts state figures in thousands of pounds (with an explanatory £'000 at the top of the column) – thus £10,000, for example, is written as 10:

	£'000
£10,000 can be written as	10

Income

The P&L account starts with all payments (sales) made into the organisation.

Sales: For a care home most of the income will be from fees paid by residents or on behalf of residents.

Additional sales: There may be a small additional income from the hire-out, for example, of the home's communal areas for seminars, meetings or functions. Or some homes offer homecare services using their nursing and care assistant resources which also provide an additional income.

Costs (expenditure):
The P&L account continues by listing all the costs by category divided into:

1. **Direct costs:** These are costs that can be completely attributed to producing the service within the care home.
2. **Indirect costs:** also known as overheads, these cannot be directly traced to producing the service; instead they are shared across the business as a whole eg admin staff salaries, rent etc.

Costs can also be categorised into variable and fixed costs:

Variable costs: These are the costs which vary depending on what is happening within the care home eg how many residents there are, whether and what activities are being offered, how many consumables (eg incontinence pads) are being used, phone bills, utility bills for water, electricity or gas, emergency repairs to the home, for example.

Fixed costs: These are costs which do not vary with the level of service provided within the care home, for example rent. However fixed costs are not always fixed in the long term as there can be an increase or decrease eg there can be a rent increase for the next year.

The profit and loss account pulls all these figures together to show whether the organisation has made a profit or a loss. Let's do it for Outstanding Quality Care Homes:

Outstanding Quality Care Homes Ltd
First Year Profit & Loss Account

	£'000	£'000
Sales		1000
Cost of goods sold		(500)
Gross profit		500
Operating expenses		
Selling & Distribution	150	
Administration	100	
Total expenses		(250)
Operating profit		250
Interest payable on loan		(100)
Profit before tax		150
Tax payable		(30)
Profit after tax		120
Dividend paid		(50)
Retained profit		70

The **income statement** starts with the receipts made into the organisation and then deducts various categories of cost, including tax and shareholder dividends. Assuming the company has been profitable, retained profit (£70,000 in the example above) can be used to fund further investment and development of the organisation or simply kept ready for a rainy day.

Abdul Sattar Edhi

Hussain

Abdul Sattar Edhi came from a humble Pakistani background and was a philanthropist, ascetic, humanitarian and man of exceptional compassion who, with his wife Bilquis Edhi, founded the Edhi Foundation. Backed entirely by private donations, the Foundation runs a network of free minivan ambulances, hospitals, homeless shelters, rehab centres and orphanages across Pakistan. By the time of his death in 2016 Edhi was registered as a parent or guardian of nearly 20,000 children. In 2013 the Huffington Post claimed that he might be 'the world's greatest living humanitarian'. Known as Angel of Mercy, Edhi was a strong supporter of religious tolerance in Pakistan and has been described as Pakistan's most respected and legendary figure.

The balance sheet

Unlike the P&L statement, the **balance sheet** is a snapshot of an organisation's financial health taken at a specific point in time, often the end of its financial year. The balance sheet is made up of **assets** and **liabilities**.

Assets are your 'goodies'. They are:

- Something the company owns like land, buildings and equipment,
- Something other people owe you – in other words something that is yours and should be in your possession but isn't at that moment. More often than not this is money, goods or services provided.

Assets are divided into:

1. **Fixed assets** which are any assets which the company uses on a long-term basis. They are assets held for use rather than for sale. They are expected to remain within the organisation for at least one year but in practice most will last much longer than this. Typical fixed assets include land, buildings (including any in the garden), lifts, nursing and bathing and lifting equipment, cars and vans and computer hardware, assuming the business actually owns them rather than leases them. Major items of software (operating systems and substantial application packages – but not usually routine maintenance) are also fixed assets.

2. **Current assets** are the assets which the company expects to turn into cash within one year eg the money from residents' fees.

3. **Intangible assets:** in some organisations and sectors there is a further asset called intangible assets. These assets have value to the organisation but it is impossible to see them and feel them like you can with fixed and current assets. Typically they include intellectual property rights (copyright, design rights, trademarks and patents). In the care home sector they also include goodwill and brand value. Intangible assets can be very hard to value.

> *We are each made for goodness, love and compassion. Our lives are transformed as much as the world is when we live with these truths."*
> *– Desmond Tutu, South African social rights activist, opponent of apartheid and retired Anglican Archbishop*

Liabilities are your 'baddies'. They are what the business owes to other people – who will normally expect to receive them sooner rather than later. Again, liabilities are usually money but not always. They are divided into:

1. **Current liabilities:** liabilities (usually money) the business expects to have to pay within the year eg money owed to suppliers.

2. **Long-term liabilities:** liabilities the business expects to pay at some stage but not within the next year eg money which has been lent to the organisation by banks.

The balance sheet brings the assets and liabilities together in one table or 'account' and then 'balances' them.

The Balance Sheet usually shows **net assets** which are what remains after the current liabilities have been removed from the current assets. Hopefully the organisation has more assets than liabilities in which case the net assets shows simply as a figure eg £100. If however the liabilities are greater than the assets the figure will be negative and is conventionally shown in brackets, eg (100).

Now let's look at the section labelled **shareholders' equity**. This section shows how the net assets are arrived at:

- **Capital invested** is the money the investors (shareholders) put into the company to get it started and later, sometimes, to help it expand or stop it going bust (and occasionally both!). Capital invested is the money the company has not earned itself.

- **Retained profit** is what the company has earned or saved itself. It is 'retained' profit because it is the profit remaining after the taxman has had his bit and dividends to shareholders have been paid.

Let's have a look at a balance sheet for Outstanding Quality Care Homes:

Outstanding Quality Care Homes Ltd
Balance Sheet as at 31 December 2017

	£'000	£'000
Assets		
Fixed Assets	1000	
Current Assets	4000	
Total Assets		5000
Liabilities		
Current Liabilities	(1000)	
Long Term Liabilities	(2000)	
Total Liabilities		(3000)
Net Assets		2000
Financed by:		
Shareholders' equity		
Capital invested	1930	
Retained Profit	70	
Total Shareholders' Equity		2000

The accounting year

Financial events and deadlines

Every organisation has an accounting period and it is normally the same 12 months as the financial year covered by their annual accounts. For most organisations this is either the calendar year (1 January to 31 December) or the fiscal year (1 April of one year to 31 March the next year).

Every business is required to keep accounts (sometimes known as accounting records) and to prepare a **company tax return** to work out how much **corporation tax** to pay if it has been profitable. This tax return is submitted to one of Her Majesty's Revenue and Customs (HMRC) offices, which one depending on where the business's HQ is situated – although many businesses now file their tax returns online and this is something the Government is encouraging. The tax return has to be submitted **12 months after the end of the company's accounting period**. If the company fails to meet its deadline it is fined

Accounting deadlines in a financial year

- **The starting point for an accounting year is the day following the end of the previous financial year, eg January 2018**
- **By nine months later (eg by 31 October 2018)** annual accounts (or abbreviated accounts) must be filed with Companies House
- **By 9 months and l day later (eg by 1 November 2018)** corporation tax must be paid to HMRC, or HMRC informed no tax owed
- **By 12 months later (eg by 31 December 2018)** company tax return must be filed with HMRC.

by HMRC. Companies who exceed a limit thought by HMRC to be significant may need to make quarterly payments on account.

Corporation tax (or a report submitted that no tax is due) has to be paid usually **nine months and one day** after the end of the company's accounting period.

Preparing the information for the annual return and the tax return and working with an independent firm of accountants (who may submit the tax return) is done by the finance director and accounts staff. You will know they are getting near the end of their year-end when they start sending you urgent requests for information. During this time they also tend to work long hours and need lots of support with tea and biscuits. It is definitely in everyone's interests for you to give them the information they need as quickly as you can.

VAT

A care home manager will, unquestionably, encounter Value Added Tax (VAT) frequently in their working (and private) lives. VAT is a notoriously time-consuming and sometimes complicated tax to administer made worse by the fact that businesses are, in effect, working as unpaid tax collectors for the government. One of the many joys of working in the care home sector, however, is that, **generally, care homes' fees are exempt from VAT**, so care home companies are not obliged to register for VAT. This exemption means that care homes do not, in most cases, have to add VAT to their residents' fees which has the effect of saving those paying the fees who are not VAT registered (ie most private clients) a great deal of money. The exemption also saves care homes a great deal of admin time and effort collecting VAT.

The disadvantage of an organisation not being registered for VAT is that it cannot claim back from HMRC VAT it has been charged itself for goods (eg lifts and hardware) or services (eg agency fees). In the VAT world life, unfortunately, is never all joy and no grief.

From this brief summary you will see that VAT has the potential to become very complicated. Should this happen, it makes very good sense for organisations to get specialist advice, and sooner rather than later.

More on VAT

A care home manager does not need detailed knowledge about VAT but it is an important tax so we have included some additional information in the Extra Info section (p114).

Self-directed reflection

Get hold of any P & L accounts or balance sheets you can and make sense of them

Notes

Budgets

What is a budget?

Why is preparing a budget important?

In Section 5 we will cover:

- ➤ **What are budgets?**
- ➤ **Types of budget**

What are budgets?

Stay calm

Many managers groan when they hear the word 'budget' but there is no need. A compassionate and commercially aware manager stays calm, gathers the information they need, does the budget and finds that a budget provides vital information about the future which, properly used, helps keep the organisation safe and provides a roadmap to the future.

For a new project, a budget is essential to prevent the project from going off on a disastrous course. Equally, it can encourage an organisation to go ahead with a product or service which could transform its fortunes.

A budget is a financial plan which helps management to keep in control of their organisation. A budget can be huge like those for massive companies like Tesco or Morrisons or for a project worth just a few hundreds or thousands. **There are two main types**:

1. **A budget for a forthcoming accounting period,** say a year. It sets goals for the organisation and provides the details needed to make the goals work. These budgets are sometimes broken down into three types:
   i. **Cap**ital **ex**penditure **(CAPEX)** budgets record the investments in the business which enable essential items like nursing beds, refrigerators and computers to be bought. These items will appear on the balance sheet as fixed items and will be **depreciated.**
   ii. **Op**erational **ex**penditure **(OPEX)** budgets focus on the everyday costs of the business (including the largest cost – which will be the staff for service businesses like care home companies).
   iii. **Sales or income budgets** focus on the money (income/turnover) being earnt by the organisation.

All three budgets should be regularly reviewed to make sure they remain in line.

2. **A budget for a specific project.** In this case **a pre-project budget** is prepared to estimate revenue, costs and the contribution the project would make towards the company profits in order to decide whether to go ahead. Once the project starts the budget provides guidelines for the managers to show how they are doing 'against budget'.

   The funds used by the company to buy or upgrade physical assets such as buildings or equipment as part of the new project or investment are recorded as **capital expenditure** (CAPEX).

   A final budget records all the financial figures and reports the extent of the project's contribution to company profits or losses.

Budgets and values

An organisation's budget can also give insight into what kind of an organisation it is. Think about your own budget and what it says about you. If you buy a lot of food, for example, it suggests either you enjoy cooking or you cannot afford to eat out in restaurants. Do you spend a lot on your house, which suggests you prefer to stay at home, or do you splash out on airlines, which suggests you love to travel? Do you spend what you earn or do you save every penny? All this financial information says a lot about what type of a person you are.

In the same way an organisation's budgets may say a lot about it. For a well-run organisation, spending a lot on training may suggest it values well-trained staff. A generous budget for fixtures and fittings may suggest it wants its home(s) to look fantastic. A generous food budget may suggest nutritious and delicious meals are an important part of its strategy. A generous marketing budget may show senior management understand how tough it is to keep a care home full.

Budgets and weaknesses

Budgets can show the strengths of an organisation as above but also its weaknesses. Here are some examples:

- **Is the budgeted income lower than last year and the budgeted costs the same or higher?** This scenario is almost always bad news. Falling income is not always bad – the company may be focusing more tightly on profitable work only – but in this case budgeted costs would also have to be down for the company to remain profitable.
- **Is the budget for the forthcoming year showing that interest paid to banks and others owed money is climbing?** This scenario would suggest rising debt may be growing into a problem.
- **Is the amount of money allocated to upgrading (eg furniture, decorations or IT) going down?** This is usually bad news because the sign of a successful company is being able to spend money on keeping ahead of the competition.
- **Has the training budget gone down?** If a company is struggling financially the training budget is often the first one to be raided. Successful companies, however, need well-trained staff so cutting the training budget is usually a bad sign.

Why do we have budgets and where do they come from?

Every well-run organisation starts with a well-thought-out strategy which outlines:

- The organisation's objectives.
- The stakeholders' ability to deliver the organisation's objectives.
- Activity planning.
- Resource planning.

The organisation then produces budgets which deliver the strategy as a necessary part of a planning course or cycle. Everything flows from the strategy and getting it right. However, if the strategy is not right, it is likely that the problems are first identified at the detailed planning and budget stage.

The budget and time frames are agreed and delivered. Having done all that preparation, delivering the actual budget or project itself is easy! (just joking).

The frequency of budgets and by whom they are delivered depends on the size and complexity of the organisation:

- Large organisations will have a main

> *Loneliness is the worst pain in this world. It constantly eats away the person's heart, and can cause the person to hate, to feel enraged. It is like a wound of the heart; the type of wounds that cannot go away with a kiss or a hug. The only thing that can make this great pain go away is love and compassion, another human heart to pull them out of this hell.*
> *– Diana, Princess of Wales*

Diana, Princess of Wales

Auguel

Diana, Princess of Wales is well remembered for her involvement in many different charities, her humanitarian work and the causes she championed. She is best known for her work on behalf of AIDS patients and towards an international ban on the use of anti-personnel landmines.

Diana's involvements in the National AIDS Trust, which researches, promotes education and the treatment of HIV/AIDS, led to a worldwide movement to establish AIDS charities. The images that became famous of her shaking hands with and touching people diagnosed with AIDS helped to change the world's perception of AIDS. Most of Princess Diana's humanitarian efforts remain active to this day.

> *Compassion doesn't, of course, mean feeling sorry for people, or pity, which is how the word has become emasculated in a way."*
> *– Karen Armstrong, English writer*

budget supervised by the Board and then each department (eg marketing) will have their own budget supervised by their head of department.

- Smaller organisations may have a single overall, main budget perhaps mini-budgets
- How often budgets are produced varies too. On the whole, the bigger the organisation the more frequent are the budgets (eg every quarter). A single care home business, by contrast, might produce annual accounts and a budget for the whole following year.
- Single project budgets are produced as required.

How much you, as a care home manager, are involved in preparing budgets varies from organisation to organisation. It is probably true that managers are much more involved now than they used to be, mainly because the importance of their commercial role is now so much more recognised. If you have been personally involved in preparing the budget for your home, it will hold no surprises for you and you can focus on hitting agreed targets.

If you have not been involved in preparing the budget, you may be placed in a situation where you believe you cannot achieve the set targets with the budget you have been given. Rather than muttering and moaning about how unreasonable your bosses are, it is always better to meet early with your line manager to discuss your concerns. Come well prepared to argue your case calmly and rationally. Hopefully good sense will be the winner and either your budget is increased or the targets reduced.

A budget is only as good as the information fed into it. So, before accepting its conclusions, you must examine carefully where the information came from, who entered it and how likely it is to be accurate. For example, if you have been asked to prepare a budget for building a new 20-bed wing for your home, you must be confident that the quotes from the builder you have chosen are accurate and your builder is not simply one of those 'best guess' builders who put in a low quote, wait until the contract is won and then suddenly discover all sorts of 'unexpected findings' which drive the costs up dramatically.

Equally important, good budgeting takes account of external factors such as:

- ☐ competitors
- ☐ national and
- ☐ local politics
- ☐ the sensitivities of the local community
- ☐ current taxation/allowances.

The full implications of the budget plans on all areas of the business must be understood as well as any impact they may have on:

- ☐ partners
- ☐ loyal suppliers and
- ☐ valued relationships.

A word of advice. If the worst comes to the worst and you go over budget, the last thing a compassionate and commercially aware manager should do is bury their head in the sand and try to pretend it has not happened. Much better is to think out carefully why the budget has been missed, what you can do to rectify the situation and how it will not happen again. If you wait until your line manager comes storming into your office demanding to know what has happened you may be in for a P45 experience.

Creating a budget

For all types of plans and budgets it is useful to start by stating the overall aims and objectives of the organisation (often called the statement of intent) and how your plan/budget is going to contribute to achieving those overall aims. You will then want to move to the specifics. Describe:

- **The key objectives** for the budget based upon your team's experience and research, the competition, local knowledge of your community and what is already changing or may change.
- **How your plans** are going to be put into practice in detail.
- **The nature and extent of the resources** needed to meet the plans. Resources are not just about cash – management time and the staff you may need, for example, are also important.
- **Prepare an initial income forecast**, based on, and reflecting, your objectives and predictions. Key income for a care home will come from:
  1. Resident fee income.
  2. Fees from any additional care activities the care home may take part in for example providing homecare or live-in care locally.
  3. Fees for the use of the premises eg fees for renting the care home meeting room or for a 'chair' for a local hairdresser.
- **Prepare a costs forecast** using the same objectives and predictions as for income forecast. Key costs will include:
  - ☐ Staff wages/salaries
  - ☐ Premises upkeep
  - ☐ Food
  - ☐ Drugs and medications
  - ☐ Consumables eg gloves, aprons, wipes, pads, towels, soaps and gel, disinfectants, cleaning products
  - ☐ Laundry products eg detergents, conditioners and bleach
  - ☐ Sales and marketing
  - ☐ Administration
  - ☐ Contingencies and emergencies.
- **Determine limiting factors for the budget:** what will stop the budget being met?
  1. Limitations of resources like ☐ not enough cash, ☐ management too stretched and ☐ appropriate staff not being available.
  2. Sales staff are pessimistic about delivering the projected sales volumes.
  3. Too few customers/clients in the area.
  4. New competition has just arrived.

The final budget

Once the income forecast is merged with the costs forecast as a single document the budget is beginning to appear like a butterfly from a chrysalis. Make sure you finish with a summary which clearly states the expected outcome of the budget.

What five features are most likely to make a budget successful?

Types of budget

Annual budget

As a care home manager you will be expected to understand your company's main budget (see p52) but will not be expected to create it.

However you may well be expected to help prepare your care home's annual budget. Let's get started! There are two ways to go about preparing your annual budget for your care home:

1. Blank-page budgeting

- **Start from scratch** with a blank page and then gradually build up your budget thinking individually about each item.
- **Start with your aims** and objectives (eg 95% occupancy in your home).
- **Decide what income you expect.**
- **Then decide what resources** (money and staff for example) you will need to achieve the expected aims and objectives as well as the expected income.
- **The advantages** of blank-page budgeting are that it is flexible and encourages both change and innovation.
- **The disadvantages** are that it is time-consuming, it can be random ('best guess') because it does not start from a proven point and it requires a detailed, expert understanding of the care home business.

2. Last year plus/minus budgeting

- This is a **more common approach** than blank-page budgeting.
- **Start with last year's income.** Decide whether fees and occupancy are going to rise or fall in which case your income will rise/fall.
- **Then look at last year's costs.** You might expect some costs to rise (eg staff) and others to fall (eg utilities) so you will need to add them all together to come up with a final costs figure.
- **Put the two figures together** and come up with the final profit/loss.
- **The advantages** of this method are that it starts from a baseline, is easier and less time-consuming, there is less chance of introducing new mistakes and it is also easier to justify to others.
- **The disadvantages** are that it can encourage a rather dull, unexciting approach to budgeting because you are always looking backwards to a starting figure, and it often ignores recent changes, both within the organisation and externally within the local community and the wider (political and financial) world.

Best practice

Some experts recommend using a bit of both the budgeting methods described. In other words, use last year plus/minus budgeting for most years with a blank-page budget every three to five years, for example, to spice things up.

Single project budgets

If you are proposing an improvement or new development which involves money you will be expected to produce a single project budget to support it. The process of preparing this budget will be almost identical to that for blank-page budgeting (as above).

Be prepared for challenges if you are asking for information and action from teams beyond your immediate team – cutting across organisations can create conflict – but persist!

Always finish with a summary which pulls the project together in terms of aims and objectives, financial information and expected outcome.

Benefits of budgeting

- **Budgets are like having excellent satnav** which helps everyone in the organisation to arrive at agreed destinations. The different routes may involve a motorway planned out by the senior management (main budget), or 'A' roads planned by heads of department (departmental budgets) or ever smaller 'B' roads set by managers at each level in the organisation (eg individual care home budgets). There may even occasionally be unmarked roads which provide an exciting ride!
- The beauty of a budget which has been prepared for you/your home is that it **provides clear guidelines for you** – focusing your attention on what needs to be done, why, when, by whom and how much money you have been given to achieve your targets.
- Budgets are **an important method of communication and co-ordination** for everyone, helping staff at the same level in an organisation (ie horizontally) and staff at different levels (vertically).
- Budgets are the means by which **managers can better control activities** through regular systematic monitoring and reporting.
- Budgets **help managers and their teams pull together** in the same direction. Budgets effectively set targets which motivate teams.

Problems of budgets

- The budget is **only as good as the information put into it**.
- The budget **may not reflect the overall strategy**, aims and objectives of the organisation – there is misfit.
- **Changing financial and/or administrative circumstances** within the organisation may make the budget inaccurate because those who have written it have failed to recognise the changes.
- When a change in circumstances has been recognised, **the change(s) is not highlighted** in the budget so their impact and significance is missed by readers.
- If the budget is too vague, **uncertainties may result** in the team failing to deliver it.
- A budget which is too detailed may cause a **lack of innovation and flexibility** in the team trying to deliver it.
- Budgets may cause low morale if they are used as a 'stick' and not as a 'carrot'.
- Budgets **can cause a silly situation** to occur where teams feel they have to spend all the money they have been given regardless of whether it is needed, because otherwise they will lose it for next year.

Negotiating budgets with managers

When preparing budgets you have to be a little bit smart because, for sure, you are going to have to negotiate them with your line manager(s). Think carefully because there are three approaches you can take using the principles and practices described above depending on the circumstances and situation you find yourself in. The three types of budget you can prepare are:

1. **The bare minimum budget**. This is the bare essentials, rock-bottom budget which offers the bare minimum and no room for

What do you think are the problems that may arise with budgeting?

negotiation (no 'wiggle room' as it is sometimes described). It describes what you think you can just about achieve. More importantly, it also describes what you cannot achieve. The level of risk is clearly spelt out. This is the type of budget you prepare when you know money is in short supply or there may not be a lot of support from management for your budget.

2. **The target budget.** This is the middle of the road budget which you would be reasonably happy with if accepted. You believe that the aims and objectives described can be achieved with the amount of funding stated. You might be prepared to negotiate a bit with your line manager but there is not much room.

3. **The luxury or 'stretch' budget**. This is a very optimistic budget, both with the expected income levels you describe and the level of costs you expect. It is the sort of budget you prepare when the organisation is doing well and you are feeling good about prospects for your care home. You are unlikely to get the full budget accepted but even if there is some 'adjustment' you will still be getting a generous budget which should please you.

Good luck with the negotiations!

Budget analysis

On page 52 is an example of a budget for Outstanding Quality Homes (capacity of 50 beds).

How are you doing against budget?

Once your budget has been agreed, **the next important step is to see how you perform** against it. The actual figures are compared with the budgeted figures usually monthly (eg when the management accounts are prepared) or more often if needed, and a running total also kept throughout the year. If they do not match there is a discrepancy which must be flagged up, explained and corrective action taken if/as necessary. The process is known as **variance analysis**.

Story

Bina was the manager of a 45-bed home in Exeter who was always looking for opportunities. She thought that the home was well positioned to provide daycare for older people living with dementia especially as she had a nice, big lounge which was hardly used at all. Her staff were well trained to care for people with dementia and Bina thought they would appreciate a change in their everyday routine. She also had a chef who was always keen to show his skill in tempting people with dementia to eat his special goodies.

Bina delivered a budget for the project to her regional manager (RM) which showed her break-even point was caring for seven daycare clients. Her budget was enthusiastically received but the RM pointed out that Bina had completely forgotten overheads like heating and lighting and her staff costs had assumed no holiday, sickness or agency-use costs. Bina adjusted her budget which now showed a new break-even point of nine clients. This budget was accepted by her company and the MD gave her approval for the project to proceed.

Bina was very disappointed that, despite her best efforts, numbers rose very slowly and quickly fell behind projections. The team persisted, though, and eventually the break-even point was reached and shortly afterwards numbers increased very quickly until they were full… and rather pleased with themselves.

What this story shows is that it is tempting to do budgets in straight lines forgetting that humans do not behave like that. No one likes eating in an empty restaurant or shopping in an empty shop ('What does everyone else know that I don't?') But the moment restaurants and shops fill up – everyone wants to be there ('Yes, this is the right place for me!'). And the same is true of joining daycare.

There are two general rules of thumb to keep in mind when looking at the results of this process of variance analysis:

1. **INCOME:** If income increases this is generally a good/positive/favourable sign, unless there is a corresponding or greater increase in costs which will wipe out any potential profit. Income decreasing on the other hand is a general cause for concern and must be thoroughly investigated to find the cause, although a corresponding fall in costs might provide an obvious explanation.

2. **EXPENSES: A decrease in expenses** is good as long as all the costs of the business has been accurately captured for the time under review. It should mean that you are making savings in your operations and this will improve your net profit. Beware, however, two situations:
    - Budgeted expenditure is not being spent or underspent. Always try to find the reason as it might cause a problem in the future. For example if the marketing budget is not spent as it should be, occupancy might start to drop quite soon.
    - There is a corresponding fall in income which means profitability stays the same.

   A rise in expenses is generally negative/unfavourable as we know we have to keep costs down if we want to make more profit. The rise needs investigation. Occasionally a rise can't be helped, for example when income is powering ahead it tends to drag up costs – but profitability too.

By doing budgetary analysis routinely, you will become more familiar and expert with your budgets, adjust quickly to any downturns, take advantage of upturns and be able to plan more effectively.

The main questions to ask yourself are:

- What is the difference between the actual and the budgeted amounts (variance). Is it good or bad as far as the company's net income is concerned?
- What impact is the variance going to make, particularly if it is negative?
- What caused the variance and is further action needed?

> *What we really need is compassion of the mind - compassion for others that is directed intelligently and produces truly compassionate results."*
> *– Harry Browne, American writer*

Using the example of Outstanding Quality Care Home's budget earlier, if we compare the actual results for the month of January to what was budgeted we can see what variance there was from the budget – see page 53.

For example we can see that there is an increase in fees of £25,000. This is favourable as income was higher than expected. The comments section allows us to analyse this and we see that the increase was not due to fees being put up but to a donation of £25,000 pounds being bequeathed to the home. This should have been entered as other income; entering it on the fees line gives us a false favourable report on fees. However it shows the net result on overall income is favourable. So maybe in order to raise more income and offset its costs the care home could consider fundraising for legacy donations.

Another example we can see that has an impact on profits is agency staff. In this case we have failed to budget for it at all and this is not good, as by itself it could have a huge impact on the profits of the company. Even though we can see that this is due to staff sickness which is unavoidable, it could have been better prepared for if a provision had been made for it. Luckily, overall the increase in this expense was offset by savings in other categories of expenses and the huge donation of £25,000 pounds to the home which resulted in a positive net variance of £22,706 on the bottom line.

By doing this analysis routinely, care home managers will become more familiar with their budgets and be able to plan more effectively and adjust for the future as they become aware of how sensitive certain items are on the bottom line.

OUTSTANDING QUALITY CARE HOME BUDGET 20XX

Registered 50 Beds

	JAN	FEB	MAR	APR	MAY	JUNE	JULY	AUG	SEPT	OCT	NOV	DEC
Days in Month	*31*	*28*	*31*	*30*	*31*	*30*	*31*	*31*	*30*	*31*	*30*	*31*
INCOME	£	£	£	£	£	£	£	£	£	£	£	£
Fees	125,206	113,089	125,206	121,167	125,206	121,167	125,206	125,206	121,167	125,206	121,167	125,206
Other income	0	0	0	0	0	0	0	0	0	0	0	0
TOTAL INCOME	125,206	113,089	125,206	121,167	125,206	121,167	125,206	125,206	121,167	125,206	121,167	125,206
PAYROLL												
Care staff	43,637	39,414	43,637	42,230	43,637	42,230	43,637	43,637	42,230	43,637	42,230	43,637
Catering	5,411	4,887	5,411	5,236	5,411	5,236	5,411	5,411	5,236	5,411	5,236	5,411
Housekeeping	4,336	3,916	4,336	4,196	4,336	4,196	4,336	4,336	4,196	4,336	4,196	4,336
Other	7,024	6,344	7,024	6,797	7,024	6,797	7,024	7,024	6,797	7,024	6,797	7,024
Agency	0	0	0	0	0	0	0	0	0	0	0	0
Holiday Pay	4,493	4,058	4,493	4,348	4,493	4,348	4,493	4,493	4,348	4,493	4,348	4,493
TOTAL PAYROLL	64,901	58,619	64,901	62,807	64,901	62,807	64,901	64,901	62,807	64,901	62,807	64,901
CARE EXPENSES												
Food	4,290	4,290	4,290	4,290	4,290	4,290	4,290	4,290	4,290	4,290	4,290	4,290
Inco products	200	200	200	200	200	200	200	200	200	200	200	200
Medical supplies	210	210	210	210	210	210	210	210	210	210	210	210
Laundry & cleaning	630	630	630	630	630	630	630	630	630	630	630	630
Waste disposal	402	402	402	402	402	402	402	402	402	402	402	402
Uniforms	116	116	116	116	116	116	116	116	116	116	116	116
Linen & Crockery	120	120	120	120	120	120	120	120	120	120	120	120
Activities	400	400	400	400	400	400	400	400	400	400	400	400
Stationary	375	375	375	375	375	375	375	375	375	375	375	375
Training	475	475	475	475	475	475	475	475	475	475	475	475
Marketing	364	364	364	364	364	364	364	364	364	364	364	364
Staff advertising	100	100	100	100	100	100	100	100	100	100	100	100
Sundry expenses	100	100	100	100	100	100	100	100	100	100	100	100
TOTAL CARE EXPENSES	7,782	7,782	7,782	7,782	7,782	7,782	7,782	7,782	7,782	7,782	7,782	7,782
FACILITY EXPENSES												
Electricity	150	150	150	150	150	150	150	150	150	150	150	150
Gas & oil	140	140	140	140	140	140	140	140	140	140	140	140
Telephone & postage	145	145	145	145	145	145	145	145	145	145	145	145
Water rates	305	305	305	305	305	305	305	305	305	305	305	305
Council tax	826	826	826	826	826	826	826	826	826	826	826	826
Insurance	575	575	575	575	575	575	575	575	575	575	575	575
Registration fees	510	510	510	510	510	510	510	510	510	510	510	510
Equipment rental	0	0	0	0	0	0	0	0	0	0	0	0
Contract maintenance	200	200	200	200	200	200	200	200	200	200	200	200
Response maintenance	2,950	2,950	2,950	2,950	2,950	2,950	2,950	2,950	2,950	2,950	2,950	2,950
Gardening	400	400	400	400	400	400	400	400	400	400	400	400
TOTAL FACILITY EXPENSES	6,201	6,201	6,201	6,201	6,201	6,201	6,201	6,201	6,201	6,201	6,201	6,201
TOTAL EXPENSES	13,983	13,983	13,983	13,983	13,983	13,983	13,983	13,983	13,983	13,983	13,983	13,983
OPERATING PROFIT	46,322	40,487	46,322	44,377	46,322	44,377	46,322	46,322	44,377	46,322	44,377	46,322
Budget occupancy	45	45	45	45	45	45	45	45	45	45	45	45
Budget occupancy %	90%	90%	90%	90%	90%	90%	90%	90%	90%	90%	90%	90%
Average weekly fee £	630	630	630	630	630	630	630	630	630	630	630	630
Payroll %	52%	52%	52%	52%	52%	52%	52%	52%	52%	52%	52%	52%
Expenses %	11%	11%	11%	11%	11%	11%	11%	11%	11%	11%	11%	11%
Operating Margin	37%	37%	37%	37%	37%	37%	37%	37%	37%	37%	37%	37%

OUTSTANDING QUALITY CARE HOMES

BUDGETED VS ACTUAL COMPARISON FOR JAN 20XX

	JANUARY BUDGETED	JANUARY ACTUAL	Variance £	Comments F= Favourable U= Unfavourable
INCOME	£	£	£	
Fees	125206	150206	25000	F: Due to legacy donation incorrectly posted in fees (see p51)
Other income	0	0	0	
TOTAL INCOME	125206	150206	25000	F: Due to legacy donation
PAYROLL				
Care Staff	43637	43637	0	
Catering	5411	5411	0	
Housekeeping	4336	4336	0	
Other	7024	7024	0	
Agency	0	2000	-2000	U: Staff falling ill. Agency fees not budgeted for
Holiday Pay	4493	4493	0	
TOTAL PAYROLL	64901	66901	-2000	U: Increase due to unscheduled agency fees
CARE EXPENSES				
Food	4290	5000	-710	U: Increase in food costs? Wastage? Investigate
Inco products	200	200	0	
Medical supplies	210	100	110	F: New supplier so better prices
Laundry & cleaning	630	630	0	
Waste disposal	402	402	0	
Uniforms	116	50	66	F: Savings due to less uniforms needing to be replaced
Linen & Crockery	120	120	0	
Activities	400	200	200	F: Less outdoor activities due to extra cold weather.
Stationary	375	250	125	F: New stationary supplier gave great discounts
Training	475	500	-25	U: Minor overspend
Marketing	364	364	0	
Staff advertising	100	0	100	F: No new staff needed so budget not spent
Sundry expenses	100	100	0	
TOTAL CARE EXPENSES	7782	7916	-134	U: Net variance care expenses
FACILITY EXPENSES				
Electricity	150	250	-100	U: Rise in electricity bill due to cold weather
Gas & oil	140	200	-60	U: Rise in gas bill due to cold weather
Telephone & postage	145	145	0	
Water rates	305	305	0	
Council tax	826	826	0	
Insurance	575	575	0	
Registration fees	510	510	0	
Equipment rental	0	0	0	
Contract maintenance	200	200	0	
Response maintenance	2950	2950	0	
Gardening	400	400	0	
TOTAL FACILITY EXPENSES	6201	6361	-160	U: Net variance for facility expenses
TOTAL EXPENSES	13983	14277	-294	U: Variance due to rise in care and facility expenses
OPERATING PROFIT	46322	69028	22706	F: All increases in expenses offset by legacy income

Self-directed reflection

From your perspective, what are the three most important points you have learnt about budgeting?

Cash and Profit/Surplus

What is the difference between cash and profit/surplus?

What is cashflow and why is it important?

In Section 6 we will discuss:

- **Cash**
- **Cashflow**
- **Profit/surplus**

Cash

Cash is money which is available immediately. It is the coins and banknotes you carry in your purse/wallet, or it is money in bank accounts, cheques and money orders. Cash is used to buy and sell goods and services. Most forms of cash are electronic these days (eg cash in your bank account), rather than held as banknotes and coins.

Cash is listed first in the balance sheet because cash is the most liquid (ie the most readily and easily used) of all of an organisation's assets.

A business is more likely to keep a large amount of cash if it routinely needs lots of cash for its everyday business (such as a betting shop). **It is less likely to keep much cash** if it has excellent financial records and an excellent cash forecasting system which enables it to invest the spare money it has with confidence knowing that this money will not suddenly be needed.

It is important for a business to know how much cash it holds, in other words how much money it has received and how much it has paid out. The problem for most businesses is that, apart from cash businesses like restaurants (lucky them), most businesses only get paid some time (eg 30 to 60 days) after presenting an invoice to the customer (the debtor). This can cause cashflow problems (see below).

Cash therefore is the lifeblood of any business because without it the business cannot operate. 'Cash is King' goes the famous saying. Sadly there have been plenty of companies (especially start-ups) making a profit who have gone bust because they did not have enough cash to pay all the day-to-day expenses.

Cashflow

Cashflow is a measure of how money flows in and out of an organisation. It is the difference in the amount of money a business has available at the end of a period (**closing balance**) compared with the amount at the beginning of that period (**opening balance**). It is positive (good news) if more money comes in than flows out and the closing balance is higher than the opening balance. It is negative (bad news) if the opposite is true. How long the chosen period is depends on the type of business. So for a newsagent the balances might be checked daily, while for a huge business like Sainsbury's it might be every three months (quarterly). The speed at which a start-up uses cash is called the **burn rate**. Lack of cash is an immediate challenge which needs solving ASAP.

Cashflow performance can be measured by something known as free cashflow. **Adjusted free cashflow** is a particularly useful measurement because it measures the amount of cash a business generates after the items below have been deducted:

- Capital expenditure.
- The cost of borrowing money.
- The purchase of specific items.
- Pension deficits.

Adjusted free cashflow as an indicator of financial performance is so important that it is usually used as a **key performance indicator (KPI).** KPIs are the measurements banks and financiers use to judge how well a business is doing.

Keeping a close eye on cashflow is therefore very important for a business or any organisation for that matter. For example many councils are now paying care homes at 60 days after being invoiced instead of the

The Dalai Lama

Christopher Michel

Tensin Gyatso was formally recognized as the 14th Dalai Lama at a public declaration in 1939.. Dalai Lamas are important monks of the Gelug school, the newest school of Tibetan Buddhism.

During the 1959 Tibetan uprising against the Chinese, the Dalai Lama fled to India, where he currently lives as a refugee and the spiritual and religious leader of the Tibetan government in exile. The 14th Dalai Lama received the Nobel Peace Prize in 1989. He has travelled the world and has spoken about the welfare of Tibetans, the environment, compassion, religion, economics, women's rights, non-violence, interfaith dialogue, physics, astronomy, Buddhism and science, cognitive neuroscience, reproductive health, and sexuality, along with various Mahayana and Vajrayana topics.

Wisdom from the Dalai Lama

- “If you want others to be happy, practice compassion. If you want to be happy, practice compassion.” – Dalai Lama XIV, *The Art of Happiness*
- “I believe compassion to be one of the few things we can practice that will bring immediate and long-term happiness to our lives. I’m not talking about the short-term gratification of pleasures like sex, drugs or gambling (though I’m not knocking them), but something that will bring true and lasting happiness. The kind that sticks.”
- “Only the development of compassion and understanding for others can bring us the tranquillity and happiness we all seek.”
- “A truly compassionate attitude toward others does not change even if they behave negatively or hurt you.”
- “Compassion is the radicalism of our time.”
- “Love and Compassion are the true religions to me. But to develop this, we do not need to believe in any religion.”
- “We can reject everything else: religion, ideology, all received wisdom. But we cannot escape the necessity of love and compassion... This, then, is my true religion, my simple faith. In this sense, there is no need for temple or church, for mosque or synagogue, no need for complicated philosophy, doctrine or dogma. Our own heart, our own mind, is the temple. The doctrine is compassion. Love for others and respect for their rights and dignity, no matter who or what they are: ultimately these are all we need. So long as we practice these in our daily lives, then no matter if we are learned or unlearned, whether we believe in Buddha or God, or follow some other religion or none at all, as long as we have compassion for others and conduct ourselves with restraint out of a sense of responsibility, there is no doubt we will be happy.”
- “When we are motivated by compassion and wisdom, the results of our actions benefit everyone, not just our individual selves or some immediate convenience. When we are able to recognize and forgive ignorant actions of the past, we gain strength to constructively solve the problems of the present.”
- “Compassion is not religious business, it is human business, it is not luxury, it is essential for our own peace and mental stability, it is essential for human survival.”
- “You must not hate those who do wrong or harmful things; but with compassion, you must do what you can to stop them — for they are harming themselves, as well as those who suffer from their actions.”

> *Nurses dispense comfort, compassion, and caring without even a prescription."*
> *– Val Saintsbury, English writer, historian, and wine connoisseur*

previous 30 days. Why? Because of their lack of cash. A payment change like this will put a new strain on your cashflow.

Cashflow forecasting

Businesses don't have to make a profit every day all the time. **Most businesses run in business cycles** so for some days or months they are taking in plenty of cash (whoopee!) but there are also lean times where very little is coming in (all that can be done is 'hang in there'). Organisations use cashflow forecasting as a way to predict the peaks and troughs in their cash balance so they can make sure they have enough cash to pay their debts during the lean months.

Instead of looking backwards as so many accounts do, the important thing about cashflow forecasting is that it looks forwards. Cash forecasting:

- can therefore predict when an organisation is going to need lots of cash.
- can predict other times when the organisation may need less cash.
- puts management more in control and less dependent on others, like banks, to get them out of trouble.

Ways to protect and speed up cashflow

- The best way to make sure you get paid on time and with the right amounts is to **build a great relationship with your customers**. For local authorities this may be the administrator responsible for payments. For private clients this may be the client themselves or relatives paying the bills or a financial organisation (like a bank) tasked with paying for the care your client is receiving.
- **Decide what your credit policy is** and stick to it. Asking clients for a deposit and for payment a month in advance suits many care homes. It is good for cashflow and it solves the tricky problem of asking for money from, say, relatives after a resident has died – something no manager wants to have to do.
- **Asking for evidence of the self-pay resident having the funds to pay** expected bills going into the future makes good sense before the client comes into your home. The last thing either party wants is for the resident to find themselves unable to pay.
- **Make sure your payment terms are fully understood** by your staff involved in 'selling' the home so that these terms are clearly and definitely communicated to those making the decision as to whether a person is going to join you. Avoid misunderstandings (real or imagined!). Payment terms would normally form part of the resident's contract.
- **Make sure your invoices are well designed** and the process of sending them out, recording and acknowledging payments and chasing late payers is the best. Sometimes it is useful to send out warning letters/emails about payments due shortly, including the amount and due date.
- **One way to help cashflow is to use factoring** (also known as invoice discounting). Factoring is where a bank or factoring company buys a business's debts (money it is owed) for, say, 90% of the debts' value and by giving the business immediate cash helps its cashflow. The factoring company then collects the debts and makes a 10% profit while the business is delighted to get its hands on some immediate cash to pay its creditors/suppliers. Factoring is commonly used in some business areas but not much in the care home sector, perhaps because care homes value relationships and factoring does not always help these. However, there may be particular reasons for your home to use factoring.

Let's have a look at a cashflow statement for Outstanding Quality Care Homes Ltd:

Outstanding Quality Care Homes Ltd
Cashflow Statement

	£'000	£'000
Operating Profit		103
Depreciation		45
Increase in stocks		-23
Increase in debtors		-85
Operating cashflow		**40**
Interest paid		-20
Dividends paid		-10
Taxation		-16
Capital expenditure		-85
Cashflow before Financing		**-91**
Financing		
Increase in overdraft	15	
Increase in loan	70	
		85
Movement/change in cash		**-6**

Profit/surplus

Profit is the difference between sales (turnover) and expenditure. Expenditure is made up of running costs and overheads. **Surplus** is the word for the same thing used by charities and not-for-profit organisations. **Profit/surplus is the best known way of measuring** how successful an organisation is, and is the information required for:

- planning and budgeting for the future.
- working out future salaries, staff bonuses and dividends to shareholders.
- deciding on future investment/reserves.
- calculating dividends for shareholders.
- working out tax liabilities.
- deciding how valuable a business is.

Profits result in a reduction in what an organisation owes, an increase in assets, and/or an increase in the owners' equity and resources for investing in future operations.

Most businesses are working to make a profit. However for many there is much more to what they do. They may wish to provide a valuable service to their community and to vulnerable individuals, please their customers, train their employees and give them meaningful work.

We would say that most care homes today feel they provide a much more valuable service

Depreciation

Depreciation is an important but quite difficult idea to grasp so don't worry if you don't get it immediately. Capital assets like nursing beds and refrigerators lose value as they age and depreciation is an accounting term which aims to describe and take account of this decrease in the monetary value of the asset(s) in the accounts.

Say it is decided that a specialist nursing bed is needed, and after negotiation it is bought for £10,000. A decision is made that the bed will need replacing after five years of use so the care home will effectively have 'lost' £10,000 over five years. This loss of value must appear in the accounts and is known as depreciation. At this point there are two main ways of calculating the depreciation. HM Revenue and Customs gives help on which type to use:

1. **Straight-line depreciation:** With this method the cost of the item bought is divided equally between the estimated years of its use. This means for the nursing bed example above that for each year for the next five years a depreciation figure of £2,000 (£10,000 divided by 5 years = £2,000) will appear in the accounts as an expense. This figure is called depreciation. For the first year therefore there is depreciation of £2,000, leaving a net book value of £8,000 which is the figure that appears in the accounts that year. Each year for the next four years there is further depreciation of £2,000 pa reducing the net book value of the nursing bed until it has no value in the accounts after five years.
2. **Accelerated depreciation:** This term is a bit of a catch-all for various different kinds of depreciation which all have in common that larger amounts of depreciation expense are charged early on in the life of the purchase and smaller ones later. This method is regarded as safer than straight-line depreciation but it can result in the accounts looking a little sad if lots of expensive items are bought at the same time.

> *Effective commissioning should recognise that reasonable profit or surplus is an essential component of effective providers' costs. Reasonable profit does not translate to 'personal financial gain': private sector providers use some of their profits to pay back their financial backers; not-for-profit providers use some of their surplus to invest in meeting their charitable or community interest aims. Any business strategy which did not aim to generate a reasonable return on investment would be unsustainable."*
> *– Institute of Public Care (2015), Market Shaping Toolkit*

ipc.brookes.ac.uk/docs/Market_Shaping_Toolkit-revised_2016

than simply making a profit. In particular we feel that most managers want to make a profit but equally important is the belief that they are providing a valuable and compassionate service to vulnerable people. The two aims go hand in hand.

Losses can quite quickly cause an organisation to run out of cash. It is this **lack of cash** to keep the organisation running which frequently forces the organisation to go bust.

Self-directed reflection

What are the five most important points you have learnt in Section 6?

Notes

Finding Clients to Fill Your Home

Think about how you and your organisation really view clients and the role they play.

Then, consider how you might change your approach to clients and how you might interact with them.

In Section 7 we shall consider:

- ➤ **Finding customers**
- ➤ **Great marketing**
- ➤ **Creating a five ★★★★★ culture**
- ➤ **Great selling**
- ➤ **Fee collection**

Finding customers

Every business has to find customers whether it is a supermarket, legal firm or restaurant. A care home manager is no different and you should learn to think of keeping your **occupancy levels** healthy (90-95% preferably) as your particular challenge at which you get really good... no, brilliant.

The first secret to becoming brilliant is to think tactically about your occupancy levels all the time – before they dip in other words. For example, work out how many enquiries you need to fill one bed and make sure you keep them coming in even if your home is full so that you are ready with a waiting list of replacements for each death or discharge.

Another example of thinking tactically is getting ready for winter by giving your residents flu jabs – they are free and recommended by doctors before the winter. Don't wait until your residents start to get flu because by then it is too late.

The second secret to brilliance is to understand that success comes from getting many different parts of your organisation to work well for you. You will need

- great marketing (see below)
- great customer care (see below)
- great selling (see below)

all working together to achieve a consistently high occupancy level.

Great marketing

Become a great marketeer

Marketing is everything that puts people into a position in which they are seriously thinking about making a purchase. It used to be about advertising and personal relationships but it is far more complicated now.

If you are part of a larger care organisation you will have a marketing department. Learn from them. Badger them. Understand why they are doing things and how your care home can benefit most.

If you work for a smaller organisation you may find you're doing the marketing yourself. First, discover if you have a marketing budget. If so, that's a good, positive start (and remind yourself to tell your boss why it should be even bigger). Research. Learn from other more experienced people. Make a plan and stick to it.

Marketing to the right people

The key to productive marketing is identifying as soon as possible those customers most likely to benefit from your product/services. This group of people is called your **target market.** This target market, though, is wider than your obvious target market, if you run a home for older people, of older people over 75 in your local community and their relatives and friends. For example, local commissioners funding local authority clients as well as hospital social workers/co-ordinators involved with discharges are very important people for you.

Great marketing is making people aware of you and your home. Remember, people don't choose a care home bed like they might a new car or a magazine. In most cases they are doing so because they absolutely have to. So great marketing is 'putting yourself out there', raising more awareness of your home than others in the area. Then...when a person suddenly finds they need to find a care home bed, your home comes immediately to the forefront of their mind. Think local community – make your care home the one that everyone in the local community thinks of. Think online and offline – there are many different awareness routes.

Tom Kitwood

Tom Kitwood was an innovator in the dementia care field. It was his aim to understand what care is like from the view of a person living with dementia. A great communicator and well known for his charisma in delivering courses and conferences, he developed inventive research projects and training courses to dispute the 'old culture of care'. He was the Leader of Bradford Dementia Group and Senior Lecturer in Psychology at the University of Bradford.

One of his major innovations was Dementia Care Mapping, an observational method for evaluating the quality of care in formal settings, which resulted from one of his first research projects. His book *Dementia Reconsidered: The Person Comes First* (1997) brought together all his work, developments and discoveries.

Where will you find your target market?

You need to build a **network of key contacts.** Suggestions for starting include ☐ social media and ☐ women's groups. And – guess what? – children have grandmas and grandpas so ☐ schools might be good places to make relationships and promote the home.

Where do frail people go? ☐ hospitals, ☐ GP surgeries and ☐ local physiotherapy practices. Who offers facilities and information to older people? Local charities like ☐ Alzheimer's Society; ☐ Age UK; ☐ churches and mosques. And don't forget to build good relationships with other local care homes – as many as one in ten referrals could come from them.

Add some more good possible marketing contacts or ideas of your own below:

A nurse is compassion in scrubs."
– Lexie Saige, pen name of American quotation anthologist and author Terri Guillemets

Don't forget geography – your target area

Your **target catchment area** is the area round your home within 30 minutes' travel by car. It is likely that over three quarters of your potential customers live within this area. Residents like to choose and live in a home which is within the area they know well. Relatives like to be able to visit easily. When doing your marketing, focus on this target catchment area in combination with your target market.

Within your target catchment area you and your home need to become very well known, you need to be visible! External marketing as suggested above is very important but you should also be **inviting your local community into your home** which you are very proud of:

- **Arrange open days** when visitors can look round, meet the residents and staff and get a feel for how excellent your home is. Prepare some residents and/or relatives who would be pleased to put their (hopefully positive!) viewpoint about the home. Be sure to feed delicious food because there are plenty of people who judge a home by the quality of the food it serves visitors.
- **Encourage local groups or people to use your communal facilities** like your lounge for meetings. Free refreshments are always welcome and create a positive atmosphere.
- **If you have a hairdressing salon** or restaurant or bar invite locals in to enjoy them.
- **Contact some local nurseries or kinder-garten schools** and see if you can arrange for some children to visit the home, preferably regularly. Then arrange for your residents to visit the nurseries. Both generations benefit.
- Take part enthusiastically in the annual **National Care Home Day.**
- **Arrange for talks** by local people on interesting local topics or get an 'expert' in to provide a wider perspective.
- **Show that you and your home are expert** in a particular area like dementia or Parkinson's disease for example so that the local community comes to you for advice and help.
- **Invite people into your home for respite/holiday/re-enablement care** for limited stays perhaps at reduced rates (justify the lower fees to the boss because it is 'marketing') so that a perfect **target audience** sees what a great home you run.

Online/internet marketing

Personal and professional referrals remain the most effective form of marketing for you but there is a further format which you must embrace enthusiastically: **online/internet marketing**.

We know that over 50% of people looking for a home either for themselves or a relative will use the **internet**. They use the internet in two ways:

1. To search for a new home which matches the amount of care they want, the kind of care they are looking for to the price they can afford.
2. To learn more about a home they have been recommended to make sure it matches their expectations.

For both the above reasons your **online offering** must be excellent. How do you achieve this?

1. **Website:** your objective, remember, is to have a website which is much better than your rivals:
   - **Domain name.** Spend time with your team and customers getting the name right. The name must be ☐ easy to write; ☐ catchy, ☐ easy to remember; and ☐ clearly linked to your home. If you find you have made a mistake with your

choice, you can always change it for a better one (this is better done sooner than later!). If you have inherited a domain name and it is clearly working for your home/customers – fine. If, however, it's clearly out of date or you discover everyone hates it then you have to bite the bullet and change it. In the long run it's important you have a name that works

- **Design/templates**. If your budget can afford an expensive design take advantage of your good luck (remembering that expensive doesn't always mean good). If not, there are plenty of cheap and effective templates (eg WordPress themes) which – with effort from you and your team – can result in an attractive website.

See www.wordpress.org for details of a version you can install on your own webspace – or you can simply buy a domain and have your site hosted for you at www.wordpress.com

- **Content**. Ask around, get advice and think carefully about what your customers want to find on your website. Your customers must be able to find the information easily (otherwise they will go elsewhere) so your priority is easy navigation not fancy design. Having a downloadable brochure is helpful for customers who may prefer the written format or wish to browse at leisure or hand the 'brochure' to someone else to read
- **Search engine optimisation (SEO)**. SEO describes the strategies, techniques and tactics used to obtain a high-ranking position from search engines such as Google and thus greatly increase the number of visitors to a website. In other words, it is important search engines can find your website quickly and easily so that it comes up first when your target market is searching for care homes in your area.
- **Update frequently**. There is nothing worse than a website which is horribly out of date. If the site was designed ten years ago then it is clearly time for an update. If the last blog posting was six months ago, visitors will not be impressed that the care home is at the cutting edge of care. Visitors want to see a modern, up-to-date site which reflects well on the home.

2. **Online directories.** These websites list care homes and provide reviews which help customers to decide which care homes to investigate. They are very helpful in driving traffic to your website so it is important you appear on them. Research to find which receive the most traffic and are therefore the best ones to choose. Most offer a standard listing for free but you might decide to take up one of their promotional packages which offer enhanced listings or banner advertising for a fee. These options offer you the opportunity to present your home in the best possible light as the best choice for compassionate and quality care.

See, for example, www.carehome.co.uk

3. **Social media.** Twitter, Facebook, Instagram, Pinterest, WhatsApp and Google+ are just

When it comes to SEO you have a simple choice:

- Either you plus colleagues do it in house and focus on making sure the key words/phrases customers are searching for (eg best care home or Birmingham or dementia garden or CQC rating) appear frequently in your web pages so that search engines find them often and therefore place your website high in the rankings.
- Or you take advice from specialist SEO experts who will advise on website structure, content, keyword research, marketing campaigns, training and reporting. Beware that 'experts' occasionally can damage your site and even reputation so they always need careful supervision.

Marketing checklist

Marketing experts use the Six Ps of Marketing:

☐ **1. Product.**
Are you totally confident about the quality of your premises?
☐ Structure ☐ Fixtures and fittings ☐ Equipment ☐ Garden.
Have you got the service you are offering right?
☐ Frail elderly ☐ Dementia ☐ Respite care ☐ Others.
Is your customer service superb?
☐ Staff ☐ Reception ☐ Marketing and ☐ PR departments;
☐ Back office ☐ Feedback.

☐ **2. Place.**
Have you placed your home at the very centre of the community?
☐ Neighbourhood ☐ Relatives ☐ Events run by you
☐ Local organisations with an interest in social and healthcare
☐ The use of your facilities free or for hire eg ☐ Meeting room or hairdressing facilities.

☐ **Keep the local press informed** about the good things happening in your home **using the four Ws**:
- **WHAT** has happened or is about to happen?
- **WHEN** has it happened or is it going to happen?
- **WHERE** has it happened or is about to happen?
- **WHO** are the key people involved?

☐ **Electronic involvement** using:
 ☐ Local and national databases and listings
 ☐ Social media and websites
☐ **Printed advertising** in local media
☐ **Radio** is a valued medium for older people and their relatives, and their journalists are always looking for good stories even if – sometimes to their surprise – they are positive about care homes.

☐ **3. Process.**
Are you totally confident about the quality of care (**the service**) you offer in the home? You must be!

☐ **4. Price.**
Have you looked very carefully at your fees?
☐ Are your fees right compared to competitors?
☐ Do your customers think your fees are right?

☐ **5. People.** What are you and your staff like to deal with?
☐ What is your annual staff turnover rate (sometimes known as **churn**) – it should be no more than 10-15% per annum
☐ Staff training needed?
☐ Could staff be better organised so everyone knows what they should be doing?

☐ What do staff, clients and relatives think about you?
☐ Are they right?
☐ Are you using **volunteers** well?

☐ **6. Plan (make a marketing plan)**
☐ Divide your plan into **five key points** about the ☐ **people** described above:
For each key point describe the most important improvements you can make:
- First describe the ☐ **action points** you are going to make
- Then put a ☐ **timescale** on the improvements eg three months
- And finally add a ☐ **budget** if needed – how much and who is going to authorise funding?

Try to be as analytical as you can with the resources you have. 'Gut instinct' is not something to be trusted regularly although it has a place occasionally. Feedback, both formal and informal, is probably a better guide for you.
☐ **Deliver** your plan based on your action points within the timescale and to budget.
☐ **Review** the success of your plan and delivery
  ☐ What have you achieved successfully?
  ☐ What remains to be done?
  ☐ Timescale of outstanding work?
  ☐ Has anything new happened which you had not thought about ?
☐ **Reflection**. What could you have done better from start to finish?
☐ **Feedback.** Despite what many marketeers would like to claim, marketing is not a perfect science and outcomes have to be constantly monitored to decide how effective the various methods have been.

Make sure your team records all enquiries about availability very carefully. **Try the useful five Ws** to make sense of the data:
☐ **What** was the enquiry about?
☐ **Who** made the enquiry?
☐ **Where** did the enquirer live?
☐ **Which** marketing stimulated the enquiry?
☐ **Why** was the enquiry made?
Analyse the data and react according to what seems to be working most effectively. Remember that effective marketing is not just about short term goals (eg getting enquiries). A longer term strategy in which you build your place in the local community is also essential.

☐ **Celebrate success**. Successful marketing is hard work and you should reward members of your team who have achieved successes. Regular rewards or prizes are good – they do not have to be massive – people just like to feel valued. For most people it's you taking the trouble which makes the difference rather than the reward itself.

Here's a great idea from bestselling author Michael Heppell: he suggests that an organisation should keep a desktop bell somewhere convenient in the main office. When anyone has a good idea or signs up a new resident or does something they are proud of, he suggests that they should give the bell a ding to celebrate their success – **and then tell everybody about it** so that everyone can learn from it. Everyone should try to ding the bell at least once a day.

You don't have to use a bell though, you can just congratulate a member of staff very publicly and give them their reward.

> *The creation of a positive organisational culture that promotes innovation and high quality has to have compassion as a central value and belief.*
> ***– Marcus Powell, Director of Leadership and Organisational Development, The King's Fund, London***

some of the most popular social media platforms which you can use to show positive stories and images of your home. Social media opens windows and makes life at your home much more transparent – which has to be good for its reputation. The key to success is frequency of use, plenty of photos (and videos if you can manage them) and content which is not obviously promotional eg forthcoming events/entertainment or interesting local facts or developments at the care home. A picture of happy residents enjoying one of your events is very reassuring to their loved ones.

But **BEWARE** – you must have an agreed policy and strict rules for social media or things can go badly wrong (see Story about Tessa, p71). All your hard work building up your home's reputation could be destroyed by just one silly mistake. We suggest:

- You must get permission first before you mention a resident or relative by name or even write something which makes it possible for them to be identified.
- There is an absolute rule that no member of staff mentions the home in any way on social media. This should be part of the staff contract. Be careful to ensure all agency staff are aware of and included in this policy.
- Only one member of staff posts so that mistakes are avoided and there is consistency and control.
- There is a clause in your insurance policy to ensure you are covered in the event of a mistake.
- And have the address of a crisis management/PR agency (eg PLMR, London) if a social media mistake is made and matters seem to be getting out of control – always contact them earlier rather than later.

Offline marketing

Print advertising is a traditional promotional medium which has worked for lots of care homes over many years so local advertising is definitely worth considering. Local newspapers and magazines are under pressure so you may be able to negotiate good ad rates. Make sure they cover your **target catchment area** with their distribution. As you will have a limited budget we suggest smaller more frequent ads rather than occasional massive ones. You want to create a feeling of recognition, permanence and stability. Remember to invite their photographer to any event you are running so you get a local feel-good news story published locally. And be sure to send news of successes the home may have achieved like winning awards (eg success in the National Care Awards) or training achievements or fun things your residents may have done.

www.careinfo.org/awards-2017/

Leaflet drops are successful because they are very well targeted. Make sure the leaflets are lively, colourful and well designed and on reasonably good paper. Delivery companies are notoriously unreliable so ask friends to look out for the leaflets popping through their front doors, and try not to pay for the delivery until you are sure they have been correctly delivered.

Local radio advertising. The radio is often neglected but if you look carefully at their demographics you will see that their listeners fit your **target market** quite well. They are not overwhelmed with advertising either so you should be able to negotiate a good deal. You might also be able to persuade them to use you as an 'expert' for commentary on controversial issues or information on social or healthcare topics (eg dementia), or accept some of your ideas for short programmes on social care.

Story

After a hard day, particularly with one resident, a care worker, Tessa, went home and tweeted her frustration. She used the resident's forename, Bob, and ended the post with 'I could kill him!!!' The tweet unfortunately got into the hands of a friend of the resident's family who, again in jest, forwarded the tweet to the family saying 'Have you seen what Tessa wants to do to Bob?!!' (Both names are changed). The family, however, did not think the tweet was funny and contacted both the police and the local media. Fortunately the matter was eventually settled without the home having to pay eye-watering damages but the reputational damage was serious. There are lots of lessons to be learnt from this story but the most important are that:

- Every worker is banned from discussing work using social media apart from one delegated person whose use of social media is designed solely to market the home.
- Every staff contract (except one and that one isn't yours) bans the use of social media about work and every worker knows about the ban.
- Your insurance covers social media.

Creating a five ★★★★★ culture

Establish the right values for your home. Getting the values right for any organisation is hugely important but expressing them is not something British managers find comes easily to them. Overcome your reservations – sit down with your staff and think about what matters most to you all. Most organisations have a mission statement which is where you can start. If not, you need to encourage senior management to produce one because it does focus the mindset of the staff. When agreed and written down, you now have a **value statement**.

The value statement should:

- **Be short** and to the point
- **Have consistent themes** such as treating your residents with respect and dignity, valuing and respecting all staff, wanting to make a contribution to the local community
- **Use key words** which describe simply your key values and empower your staff. Such words might include:

☐ Excellent	☐ Award-winning
☐ Brilliant	☐ Caring
☐ Compassionate	☐ Friendly
☐ Truthful	☐ Forward-thinking
☐ Hard-working	☐ Community-spirited.

Your value statement should then be **distributed to all – repeat all – staff** using texts, emails and social media. It should be printed and stuck on notice-boards in the staff room and be made available at Reception. You can talk about your values informally or formally in meetings, staff appraisals and interviews. It is important all the staff – not just management – buy into the values and feel comfortable with them. They will then be much more effective at selling the home, whatever their role.

Making a good first impression

1. **Encourage your staff to smile.** It is amazing how important this small act is.
2. **The first interview with the client/relative is very important.** You clearly want to wow every potential client/resident all the time in every interview. One interesting approach is taken by Michael Heppell in his book *Five Star Service* in which he suggests that the most successful strategy is to use a series of '**wee wows**'.

Combine them together and they become "Simple ideas which go a long way to making a big difference in how our customer perceives us".

Here are some suggested 'wee wows' to put into practice in your interview with the client:

- ☐ Be on time
- ☐ Listen carefully
- ☐ Smile
- ☐ Show you are confident about your home
- ☐ Makes notes about the potential client
- ☐ Say please and thank you
- ☐ Be positive
- ☐ Be considerate
- ☐ Tell the truth
- ☐ Establish eye contact immediately
- ☐ Have a firm handshake
- ☐ Do what you say you will do
- ☐ Personally follow up the interview.

Perhaps you might like to write some more of your own 'wee wows' below

Brands

A strong **brand** is what many organisations crave – think of Heinz, Ford and Amazon. The value of brands in the care home sector has been much debated. A strong brand can be very helpful because potential customers – especially purchasing departments in local authorities – recognise strong brands and link them with good quality care. If you work for a larger company it is quite likely that they have an external PR company or internal PR department working on marketing including brand development. Keep in close touch – two-way communication traffic is best. They are often enthusiastic people who will appreciate your enthusiasm.

So a strong brand usually means more business. The only problem with the care sector is how quickly a brand can turn sour. Just one safeguarding incident or perhaps reports of an abused resident in a branded home can immediately damage the reputation of all homes with the same brand and it can take years for people's memories to fade. This is known as **cross-contamination.** It definitely presents a challenge.

If your home belongs to a smaller group or is a singleton you are unlikely to be asked to focus on a brand but rather the name and reputation of your home. Your objective will, therefore, be the same – to become known locally as a popular and well-respected home. It's true you won't benefit from the referrals that a strong brand brings but at least you won't suffer from the knock-on effects of poor publicity for a brand caused elsewhere should that occur. Bad publicity online sticks around for a particularly long time.

Story

Hollyoaks was a residential care home in the Midlands which was stuck on occupancy at the 85% level. The manager, Sandra, was looking for ways to push it up beyond the 90% mark. One day a care assistant in one of the sitting rooms heard the daughter of a resident say, "This would be a lovely room for our club to play bridge in." The care assistant thought a bridge club might be a great opportunity for the home (perfect target audience) and spoke with Sandra. In no time the home had 20-30 people playing bridge every Wednesday. The players learnt what a lovely home Hollyoaks was and six weeks later the uncle of one of the players moved in. Several relatives and friends moved into the home over the next year solving the occupancy problem and creating a great community. For added jam – a niece of one of the players joined the home as a care assistant.

This was an excellent example of opportunistic marketing and it didn't cost a penny – apart from the free biscuits and teas and coffees for the bridge players!

Great selling

Selling is the process of getting an individual to commit to buying – closing the deal as they say in the US. Don't be half-hearted about selling your home if you are truly proud of it. After all, your new client will receive great care and will benefit from living in your amazing home so it's win-win all round.

Getting a potential client to commit to taking a room in your care home is the ultimate sales achievement for you and your team. To reach this pinnacle takes a lot of effort, experience, excellence and energy including:

- Brilliant marketing to persuade clients to visit your home.
- A home which is truly person centred and compassionate and makes a really positive impression from the start.
- Well cared-for residents who are your best spokespeople.
- Articulate relatives who love your home and are prepared to speak up for it.
- A well-conducted interview and walk-round with the potential client/relative(s).
- Superb staff who are well trained and understand that every one of them is a sales person.

A person-centred, compassionate home

- **First impressions count.** When you next visit a supermarket take a look around the entrance. You will find fresh fruit and vegetables because they make us feel this is a healthy place which deserves our support. Why also flowers and freshly-baked bread? Because they smell good and put us in the right mood to buy. Apply the same principles to your entrance. This is going to be your potential client's home so make the entrance look homely – no tired looking notices.
- **A well-run reception** is important for admin purposes but don't let it dominate the entrance to your home causing potential clients and relatives to feel they are coming into an institution.
- **A well-run walk-round and interview** (see below) is essential to show how good your home is. Only staff members who have been specially trained should be doing such a vital part of the sales process. It is important you/they have rehearsed what you/they are going to say at each stage so that every positive point is made passionately and

sincerely. But do not allow what you have to say to become too obvious and monotonous. Customers have a knack of spotting a script and don't appreciate being treated as 'just another punter'.

Well-cared-for clients

A compassionate and commercially aware manager will know that clients who are:

- ☐ looking healthy
- ☐ well-dressed
- ☐ active
- ☐ interested

are the best possible advertisement for their home. Sometimes it is possible to involve clients (perhaps supported by relatives and/or staff) to help by giving first-hand accounts of what it is like to live there. Clients who can be seen to be clearly living fulfilled lives in every sense will encourage prospective clients greatly. Think about ☐ activities ☐ spiritual needs ☐ privacy ☐ individual food likes and dislikes ☐ relationships with staff and relatives/friends.

Supportive relatives

Supportive relatives and volunteers are your best salespeople for reaching the local community. Eighty per cent of your potential clients will live within half an hour's drive from your home so this is your target community and you need ambassadors out there recommending your home.

Just as there is nothing better than supportive relatives, there is nothing worse for your reputation than relatives slagging off your home. So keep a close eye and ear out for anyone who may not be happy about your home. Occasionally relatives behave so badly that the most appropriate way forward is to terminate the resident's placement. Very occasionally such steps may also be needed if you cannot provide what the resident needs. To protect yourself (recent legislation has put you at greater risk) and the home make sure – with legal advice – that your resident contracts cover both these scenarios. If all else fails you may need to resort to involving the courts: get early legal advice first.

Your staff are a key part of your sales force

It is vital that every staff member at every level and in every department knows that they are an important member of your sales staff. There will be designated staff who do the formal 'selling' but everyone is on show and contributes to a successful team:

- **Every staff member should receive some sales training** so they understand the importance of all the stages involved. Some homes feel that using the word 'sales' with staff can scare them and they prefer alternatives like 'customer service'. Whatever the words used, it is important that staff value the sales process and understand how important it is to the future of the home.
- **Staff members should understand they are selling the home all the time** in the way they behave with ☐ clients; ☐ relatives and visitors; ☐ other staff members; ☐ professional visitors including inspectors; ☐ suppliers – in effect all **stakeholders** (see page 23).
- **Away from the care home staff can be fantastic salespeople** at conferences, workshops, exhibitions, awards (eg National Care Awards) and in their own social life of course. But it is worth providing them with guidelines as to what it is appropriate to say on these occasions.
- **It is worth warning staff when sales walk-rounds are due** to take place so they are prepared. This could be because sales walk-rounds always take place at a certain time eg every Tuesday morning. Alternatively staff hand-overs can be a good time to warn everyone to be ready for a walk-round that day.
- **Every telephone call to the home could be a sales-related call.** So you need to make sure every staff member receives telephone training and understands that the way they answer every call could be the difference between welcoming a new client to the home – or not.
- **Make sure the contact details of all sales**

leads are taken and a walk-round appointment offered. Hopefully this offer is taken up but if it is not you or other senior member of your team should follow up the lead by explaining that as a senior member of the team you are keen for them to visit the home and asking what you need to do to make this happen. It is likely that other homes are being visited at the same time and you do not want potential clients to think that you are not very enthusiastic about them joining you.

- Once the walk-round appointment is booked **send the potential client excellent information** about the home and then make sure they are rung a couple of days before the appointment to confirm they have understood the information and will be keeping the appointment.
- During this early contact with a potential client **you should practice – and encourage your staff to practice – a holistic approach** in which you first get to understand the person, their needs and those of the person considering coming into the home (sometimes different). The facts, figures and transactions can come later once trust and confidence has been established.
- **You must have at least one member of staff who is responsible for recording all client leads** and outcomes. It is essential you know how successful you are with your leads overall and which approaches are best. Some care homes reward a member of staff who has clearly helped a client to commit to booking a room.
- **Some care homes appoint specialist outsourcers** to handle their marketing and enquiries. If yours does, do not imagine that is the end of your responsibilities in this area. They will need checking (eg by you and by mystery shoppers) and supervising to ensure they deliver the service they have promised and you are paying for.
- One sales opportunity which we think is missed by many homes is the **'emergency admission' from hospitals at the weekend**. Many homes feel that their lower weekend staffing levels and lack of senior staff do not equip them to accept such admissions. However we feel that hospitals are always under huge pressure to find emergency beds at short notice and that if a home has a policy of accepting clients at weekends which is well promoted to hospitals, it will benefit enormously. Such a policy does, however, require a change of approach to staff at weekends. Worth some local research perhaps.

> *Begin doing what you want to do now. We are not living in eternity. We only have this moment, sparkling like a star in our hand – and melting like a snowflake."*
> ***– Francis Bacon Sr., English philosopher, essayist and statesman***

Dealing with an awkward customer

- **Listen carefully** to what the customer says because awkward customers rarely get listened to and appreciate anyone who does listen. Sometimes they have a good point to make.
- **Reinforce your listening** by nodding repeatedly, repeating key phrases or pieces of information and smiling occasionally.
- **Make notes**. It is surprising how awkward people feel put off their stride by note-taking and especially if, after an appropriate time, you close your notebook with a snap saying, "That's very helpful. Thank you."
- **Some people feel they need to 'vent'** (express their anger). After a while venting they may feel rewarded, fall silent and reward your patience by going away.

Turn complaints into positives

No one enjoys complaints but you can turn them into a positive. After all, they might be right! Ignorance is not bliss when it comes to being unaware of how your clients feel.

Nothing is worse than a silent client with a grievance. If you feel a client or potential client is unhappy it is best to encourage them to tell you their concerns because it makes them feel better and gives you the best opportunity to put the problem right.

To turn a complaint into a positive you should:

- **Deal with the complaint quickly** – a lingering complaint can quickly become a marketing nightmare.
- **Always meet with the person making the complaint yourself**. If this is impossible for some reason, delegate the task to a senior member of your team who, preferably, has had training. Complaints are not for inexperienced staff. Try to meet in person avoiding emails and social media which can so easily make everything sound worse than is intended.
- **You must be truthful in your replies** and if you don't know an answer, say so – but promise that you will get back to them very shortly with the answer. Be sure to do so.
- **Use positive words or phrases in your discussions,** for example:
  - **"I am so sorry. I know how you feel…"** is a great way to show your customer that you understand what they are experiencing and will do your best to make it right.
  - **"In the past I have found…"** is a great way to show that you are experienced and are likely to make a workable suggestion.
  - **"In my experience…"** is another reassuring phrase to use.
  - **"That's a great question…"** compliments the questioner and makes them much more likely to accept your answer.
- **Accept criticisms graciously** as 'useful feedback' and if they are justified make sure you do what is needed and the client knows you have done so.
- **Keep a record of all complaints and how they were fixed** so that future staff never make the same mistakes again.
- And remember that **there is no better ambassador** for your home than a person whose complaint has been successfully fixed.

There is debate as to whether you should make it easy for people to make complaints. Some experts argue that the very fact you are encouraging this feedback is reassuring for residents living in your home and potential clients because it suggests you are always looking to improve. Others, however, think that drawing attention to complaints is a mistake since it immediately introduces the idea that complaints happen in your home commonly enough to get a special mention. You will have to make your own mind up on this one!

Feedback

Please find below some questions you might include in your feedback form. Suggest that the respondent scores you out of five with '1' as very poor moving to '5' as very good:

- ☐ Were we enthusiastic when you made contact?
- ☐ How easy was it to arrange a visit?
- ☐ Did you find the quality of the fittings and furnishings of our care home met your expectations?
- ☐ Did you find the level of service offered to residents met your expectations?
- ☐ How impressed were you by the staff?
- ☐ How easy did you find us to deal with?
- ☐ How helpful did you find your visit?
- ☐ Was there any information which you would have liked which we did not supply?
- ☐ How did you learn about us? Please put a circle round your best answer below:

Friend/Relative	GP Practice
Hospital referral	Website
Local press	Other

Fee collection

Getting the basics right. Because resident fees are pretty well your only income it is fairly obvious that your organisation needs to have an efficient system of collecting them. This manual is not the place for a detailed guide but here are some suggestions:

Review your system of fee collection

Every care home/care group will have its own methods of setting, collecting and recovering fees. It is always worth reviewing this system to decide whether it is working as well as it should be. **This review should include:**

- ☐ **Are you and/or your administrators totally confident** that your policies (including terms and conditions) are fair, legally sound, enforceable and appropriate?
- ☐ **Have you and your admin support staff received training** and are you confident that you are well prepared to cope with funding challenges?
- ☐ **Does senior management** and/or Head Office give you the support you need?
- ☐ **Should a fee prove difficult to collect** are there clear, written guidelines about the action you and your team need to take, or are there arrangements in place for others to take on this demanding task?
- ☐ **Do you have, readily available, legal support** which can be quickly authorised?
- ☐ **Are minutes of all meetings** as well as written records of any action taken kept safely for a future manager to rely on if needed?

Sensitivity, compassion and clarity

The day a client comes into your home is a huge moment for them, their family and carers so it is vital the moment is handled with sensitivity and compassion. It is not the best moment to be discussing financial matters so these should be agreed in a business-like manner well before the resident joins you. When residents are admitted as an emergency, the priority is getting them well settled, but agreement about the basics of how they are going to be funded must not be forgotten.

While always being considerate and compassionate these are some of the important commercial facts which need to be established:

- ☐ **Who is funding the resident?**
- ☐ **If the resident is self-funding**, how are the fees being funded? Are all the benefits due to them being paid (eg Attendance Allowance, Disability Living Allowance / Personal Independence Payment (Care Component) and Severe Disability Premiums) Are there back-up plans in place should the needs of the resident change or if the funding runs out?
- ☐ **If the resident is being funded by the family**, how are the fees being funded? Again, are there back-up plans in place should the needs of the resident change or if the funding runs out?
- ☐ **If the resident is being publicly funded**, have all the terms and conditions been agreed? What is the agreed position about top-up payments?
- ☐ **What is the status of the resident** – have they been assessed as needing, for example, continuing healthcare, nursing care, respite care, re-enablement care etc?
- ☐ Does the resident/family have access to **good, independent financial and legal advice?**

Legal, legal, legal

The many rules and complications surrounding fees, contract cancellation, top-ups, deferred payments, assessment under the Care Act 2014, payment/procedure during hospital stays, notice periods, recovering unpaid fees etc etc mean that you must be well prepared. For example:

- **From the start you must ensure residents have the mental capacity** to make legal decisions. If there is any doubt you must seek expert guidance. Remember too that your residents' capacity may change with time and you need to keep up to date. If the resident does not have full mental capacity you need to have full details of the person who does.
- **You are required by law to have a contract/resident agreement** with all self-funders. If CQC discovers that you have not made such an agreement with a resident you may be served with an enforcement notice.
- **Template letters are a great support for managers**, helping you to remember details you might otherwise forget and also providing a basis for conversations with potential residents, with families, local authorities and commissioners
- **It is a good legal principle to get help sooner rather than later, if you think you may be out of your depth legally.**

Self-directed reflection

From what you have learnt in this section, write below at least five must-do points which you are going to action immediately – yes, immediately!

Your Staff, Your Team

How does your organisation organise its staff? What are its strengths and weaknesses?

What are the best ways to build a brilliant team?

In Section 8 we will discuss:

- ➤ **What an organisation looks like inside**
- ➤ **Building a fantastic team**
- ➤ **Interviewing**
- ➤ **Retaining staff**

What an organisation looks like inside

Staff

Most managers agree that staff are their most important asset. To be successful, a compassionate and commercially aware manager needs to know:

- how staff are organised and therefore how to go about getting help and support when needed.
- how to build the best team and retain them.

How senior staff are organised: the Board

The person in overall charge at the top of a business is the **managing director (MD)** or the **chief executive officer (CEO).** The key word to notice here is **executive** because an executive within an organisation is an employee paid by the organisation to work for it, whereas a **non-executive** is an adviser brought in to help part-time, and who may have roles in other companies. In smaller organisations the owner is often also the CEO.

The MD/CEO is helped by a **Board of Directors** including a **Chairperson.** The Chair is usually a very well respected person and is senior to the CEO. This seniority is important because it is the Chair who would sack a CEO who was not performing (although the Chair might be wary of sacking the owner – the compliment might be returned!). The Chair is usually a non-executive who has a broad, strategic vision and role to keep the organisation heading in the right direction.

The Board of Directors is usually made up of **executive directors** who run the organisation and some **non-executive directors** who often bring specialist expertise or contacts to help. Typical executive directors include a **finance director (FD)**, sometimes called a **chief financial officer (CFO).** The FD, who usually has an accounting background, is responsible for running the financial side of the company. In many care homes companies there may be a **chief operating officer (COO)** who is responsible for the day-to-day running of the homes. There may be a **commercial director**, responsible for marketing the homes and for occupancy, and bigger organisations will also have a **human resources (HR) director** who is responsible for recruiting, training and, sadly, firing staff when needed.

The **non-executive directors** often have either executive or non-executive roles within other organisations and may have specialist skills which are particularly helpful to the organisation. For example, a non-executive director may have expertise in dementia or mental disability or be able to help improve the IT systems across all the homes.

Regional directors and heads of department

Immediately below the Board are the **regional directors** and **departmental heads.**

The key regional director is the **regional operations director (ROD)** who usually has responsibility for a number of homes grouped geographically for ease of use or occasionally by specialty eg learning disabilities. The ROD has typically been a manager themselves and is an excellent source of knowledge and problem-solving. Sometimes they are given responsibility for homes with poor occupancy or safeguarding issues or poor inspection reports or lack of staff, all of which present special challenges to their managerial and commercial skills. They usually report to the COO.

Departmental heads are important people too within larger organisations. They are responsible for the smooth running of their department which is usually based at the organisation's HQ. The **financial controller**, for example, runs the finance department on a day-to-day basis and reports to the FD.

Professional advisers

Sometimes care home managers benefit greatly from the support of **management and professional advisers**. Law firms, accountancy firms, PR and marketing consultancies, IT consultancies, advertising agencies, for example, can all be very helpful but the most important point is that they are already familiar with the care home sector and have a proven track record which has been personally checked – not just trusted – before they start working. Local builders in particular need close supervision!

The key management – you

Care home managers – you – are key people in a care home company. Upon your collective skills depends the future of the company. A terrible manager can ruin a high performing care home within six months, and equally a brilliant manager can transform a disaster into a huge success – although, as is the tough way with the world – it may take longer to do so. You have to be multi-skilled, working with senior management, your own team, your residents and relatives, volunteers, inspectors and other professionals sent to review the home. How do you do it?

Start with yourself

'Know thyself' is a phrase which was carved into the Temple of Apollo at Delphi in Greece hundreds of years before Christ was born. Even then the Greeks understood that everyone needs to know their strengths (and build on them), and weaknesses (to try to reduce them). There are many different ways to help you, from religion to mindfulness (see p116), or management courses, for example. This manual is not the place to explore this aspect of your professional and personal life but it is something you should think about. So many organisations are over-managed and under-led. You need to be a leader whose personal example has the ability to inspire and influence everybody in your team.

Arian Zwegers

The Temple of Apollo at Delphi

Make sure you have a great people management system

In the past, managers (or their line managers) could make excuses about the quality of their human resources management systems because they were often expensive and difficult to work. New easy-to-understand software and the arrival of cloud technology, however, has changed all that and there are no excuses left. Cloud-based HR systems can now cost as little as £2-3 per employee per month and provide you with the instant info you need. They should be able to:

- **Store and manage key employee information** as well as including important additional information, such as dates of birthdays and reviews.
- **Store important documents** in secure storage areas.
- **Track employee timekeeping.**
- **Log appropriate health details** and sickness records for employees.
- **Provide you with instant staff holiday info** which allows you to make quick, informed decisions about holiday requests.

A good HR system should be able to provide you with an overview which will allow you to track staffing trends and even spot future problems. You can't ask for more than that!

Building a fantastic team

The keys to building a fantastic team include:

1. **Winning buy-in from your staff.** In the past, teams tended to have a pyramidal structure with the boss at the top telling everyone what to do, helped by layers of people all of whom were very protective of the position they held. Nowadays structures tend to be flatter and more flexible with staff at all levels being empowered to stretch themselves and do what they can. So, be a true leader and don't be threatened by other people taking responsibility – in fact, actively encourage it. If you involve your staff, they are more likely to buy into what you are trying to achieve and the whole team will be more successful than just you battling away on your own. Here are some suggestions to help:
   - ☐ **Ask your staff** what they think could be improved. Sometimes you will be amazed at what you hear, for example from the housekeeper or chef who may, wrongly, not see themselves as being at the 'centre' of the home and therefore not able to say what they think without encouragement from you.
   - ☐ **If a member of staff, or a team, is having difficulty** with some aspect of their work, help them by doing it with them but never do it for them.
   - ☐ **Involve your staff** in their training – everything from its value to how best it suits individuals to learn. And don't forget the simple value of mentoring (getting a more experienced person to help starters) and coaching (getting the trainer to ask questions which make people think rather than simply providing answers).
   - ☐ As far as possible persuade everyone in the home that **they should be involved in decision making**. This helps both buy-in from the staff into the decisions and team unity.
2. **Look after your staff and their physical and mental health:**
   - ☐ **Physical health**: Some operators encourage in-house exercises (eg step-ups or sit-to-stand exercises) which can be done by busy professionals during the working day. Others offer subsidised subscriptions to local gyms, or pedometers so staff can measure how far they have walked every day. Encouraging healthy eating is also important (provide fresh fruit rather than biscuits) and regular checks of blood pressure, blood cholesterol and body mass index.
   - ☐ **Mental health**: Staff in care homes often find themselves in emotionally-charged situations all of which can lead to a gradual build-up of stress and a feeling of helplessness, exhaustion and overwork. Managers need to be on the look-out for symptoms and be ready to support an affected staff member by suggesting, for example, telephone helplines, in-house counselling or referral to their GP.
   - ☐ **Compassion**: We hear the phrase 'compassion fatigue' increasingly often, suggesting there is only a limited amount of compassion a person is capable of before becoming overwhelmed. There is an alternative view. Findings from recent research studies suggest that compassion can play a significant role in reducing physiological stress and promoting physical and emotional well-being. In fact, compassion can help us become more resilient, it can allow our natural instinct to care for another human to strengthen us not overwhelm us Developing our capacity for compassion makes it possible for us to help others in a more skilful and effective way.

For studies and articles on the benefits of compassion, see the Center for Compassion and Altruism Research and Education, Stanford University), http://ccare.stanford.edu

3. **Arrange for some or all your staff members to 'be a resident'** for a day at least so they can experience what it is like to live in a care home as a resident. This is often called 'learning by experience'. The staff member is treated like all the other residents including explaining their likes and dislikes. The staff member learns from this experience how apparently small choices make a big difference to their life (eg food choices and toileting) and the staff learn how well (or badly) they carry out residents' wishes.

4. **Make family carers feel part of the team.** Family members often have expertise in the care needs of the person they have previously been supporting. Encourage your staff to value this expertise and to use it. There will be benefits for the carers, the residents and the staff. CQC guidance is clear that visiting by relatives and joint activities with friends and relatives of residents should always be encouraged. Very occasionally you may feel that a visitor poses a risk to residents and staff. In these circumstances you will need to proceed with great caution – there is CQC guidance but you may feel you need to seek legal advice as well.

5. **Make volunteers feel part of the team.** Volunteers can make a huge difference to a home but do not imagine that it is an easy task to make their involvement work well for everybody. It is a skill which you – but preferably a senior member of your team – has to learn.

www.ncvo.org.uk/practical-support/volunteering/volunteering-in-care-homes is a good place to start and My Home Life (www.myhomelife.org.uk) also has some excellent tips on how to make care home volunteering work.

6. **Share and celebrate good practice** with the team. Make clear to the team how it was achieved.

7. **Share, frankly, what has gone wrong**. Try to do it in a 'no blame' way where people are not blamed for mistakes but, rather, put the emphasis on how the team learns from mistakes and improves.

Andy Bradley

Andy Bradley created Frameworks 4 Change (F4C) in 2004, with the "mission to create and sustain consistently compassionate caring environments for older people (including those with dementia), people with mental health issues and people with learning disabilities". Growing up, he spent considerable time living in the care home set up and run by his parents. F4C helps care providers to develop a reflective and values-led culture which show that everyone matters and to promote the qualities of care which matter most to people. Andy's vision is for the growth of compassion in all health and social care in the UK. In 2012 Andy was named one of Britain's 50 New Radicals by Nesta and The Observer. In the same year he gave a TEDx talk on the topic 'Closing the Compassion Gap'. Andy speaks in the UK and internationally on mindfulness and compassion in care.

> *The best teachers offer lessons about "determination, aspiration, resilience and compassion".*
> *– Prince Harry, younger son of Prince Charles and Princess Diana of Wales*

8. **Think about introducing mindfulness** concepts to you and your team. Mindfulness is increasingly used by management to increase mental calmness, awareness and resilience. For further info go to the Extra Info section (see p116).

9. **Provide a budget** for new ideas and opportunities. So often, good ideas go nowhere because neither money nor time is allocated. Often just a few pounds, and lots of enthusiasm, will go a long way.

10. **Delegate, delegate, delegate.** You can't do everything and more importantly, you shouldn't want to. Learn to pass on some tasks which a member of your team could do instead – with help from you. Successful delegation is in everyone's best interests:
    - ☐ **The manager's best interests**: Time management – putting your priorities first – is really important. By delegating successfully you are able to use your time better and are therefore able to think about future goals, not just spend your time doing routine tasks. You will also find that your overall performance and health improves and you will earn the respect and loyalty of your team by giving them responsible tasks which increase their sense of being valued.
    - ☐ **The team's best interests**. Team members learn new skills under your supervision. The trust and confidence you have shown in them raises their self-esteem which, in turn, helps them achieve other goals. The delegated tasks make their work more interesting and having been given greater responsibility they will start to use their own initiative and imagination more. Your team will feel appreciated.

11. **Feedback.** A team won't become fantastic without feedback. One way is to organise staff surveys, say once a year. It's true they are time-consuming but they often give you valuable – and sometimes surprising – information you won't get any other way. They also show the staff you are interested in their views. Make sure you use the feedback! Giving positive feedback is easy – everyone enjoys giving and receiving praise. It's the negatives which can be difficult because no one enjoys giving – or receiving – negative feedback. Here are some ideas for giving constructive criticism:
    - ☐ **Use what is known as a 'praise sandwich'** for giving negative feedback. In other words, give some positive feedback, then the negative

Some ideas to make delegation more successful

- **Make sure you choose the right person** for the task. Does the person have the right experience and attitude?
- **Describe the task carefully** and simply. Sometimes it is worth getting your colleague to tell you what she understands she has to do so both of you are clear and confident
- **Make sure the person knows** what the outcome of the delegated task is expected to be
- **Watch while the person starts** the task but leave as soon as it is clear she is going to be fine
- **Build on success.** Once the person has mastered one new task, make sure she feels confident and then consider building on the success and see **what other tasks** might be suitable for her
- Is the person, in time, going to be **suitable for promotion?**

and finish the sandwich with the positive.

- ☐ **Never criticise someone on the basis of gossip or speculation**. Your feedback to a member of staff must be based on fact and always be constructive with the sole purpose of trying to help the member of staff.
- ☐ **Try to criticise someone on the basis of what they have done** (''You were rude'') rather than on the basis of who they are (''You tend to say nasty things to everyone''). Feedback is designed to improve what people are doing rather than trying to change their personalities.
- ☐ **Don't overload the bad news.** Stick to one point and keep it short and simple.

Interviewing

Interviewing for great staff

Staff leave every home so do not despair if they leave yours too. There will be all sorts of reasons they leave – financial, personal, familial, geographic, health – beyond your control. For these reasons **staff 'churn'** (the percentage of total staff leaving and being replaced every year) varies greatly from home to home. The key question for you is whether they are leaving your home in greater numbers than they should be. You should seek guidance from your line manager as to the past performance of your home but in the most general terms if your home has a churn rate of under 10% (ie less than one in ten staff members are leaving every year) you are doing fine. On the other hand if the rate is more than 30% and one in three staff members is leaving every year, you have a challenge.

One of the best ways to cut your churn rate is to employ the right people in the first place. **Successful interviewing for staff** is not a matter of hoping for the best. **It requires great skill and needs:**

Careful preparation and homework

Spend twice the time on homework as on the interview. Don't kid yourself you are doing the homework if you are not – it will turn out badly. Spend time deciding exactly what your needs are and how those needs are going to be met by the person you are looking for.

- ☐ **What exactly is the post** being offered?
  - ☐ **What is the nature** of the work?
  - ☐ **What experience** is needed?
  - ☐ **What qualifications** (if any) are required?
  - ☐ **Pay**
  - ☐ **Terms and conditions**
  - ☐ **Probation period**
- ☐ **What type of person** do you want in the post?
- ☐ Have you made sure that **information about the post** is fully available to the candidates? Is it available:
  - ☐ At the care home?
  - ☐ At the agency?
  - ☐ On the website?
- ☐ **Who** is interviewing with you? Have the interviewers decided what questions each one is going to ask all the candidates?
- ☐ Should you **involve a resident** in the interviewing process including selecting the short-listed candidates from the applications? Many homes now do, so you would not be doing anything unusual or likely to cause you problems if you did. If you do include a resident on your interviewing panel and they have a diagnosis of dementia make sure there is someone on the panel able to intervene quickly if the person with dementia asks questions which they do not realise are inappropriate for the interview.
- ☐ **How long** is the interview? Do you have to decide on a **'winning' candidate** immediately?

- [ ] Have you made absolutely sure that **all the short-listed candidates are able to work legally** in the UK? The Immigration Act 2016 has introduced new penalties for illegal workers and employers who know, or have reasonable cause to believe, that an employee does not have permission to work in the UK. The Act has lowered the bar from actual knowledge that an employee was working illegally to 'reasonable belief' which is a significant development. Penalties for employers have risen to a prison sentence of up to five years (previously two) and a fine of up to £20,000. Persistent offenders could have their care home closed by immigration officers for up to 48 hours. It is likely that penalties will continue to increase.

Successful interviewing

When it comes to recruiting care staff, **values** are key. Care skills (and very important they are too) can be taught but values are what you should be looking for. Compassion, kindness, a caring nature, a desire to help are difficult to teach in a classroom.

Also important in staff is what is known as emotional intelligence – the ability to recognise and respect what is important to other people, to be able to manage social difficulties, tensions and challenges successfully, and to understand the effect each of us has on others as well as our own failings.

It has become increasingly routine to ask all candidates the **same questions** to be fair to all. But that doesn't mean the questions themselves have to be routine. And try to make the interview a conversation not an interrogation so use follow-up questions to put the candidate at ease.

> *Only choices made in love are compassionate. There are no exceptions. Do you have the courage to act with an empowered heart without attachment to the outcome? If not, you have no ability to give or experience compassion. That is the shocking truth.*
> ***– Gary Zukav, American author***

Use your EARS

There's a useful acronym for successful interviewing called **EARS:**

E for Engage – look people in the eye, nod and smile to show you are listening and understanding

A for Ask – all the questions you wanted (as above)

R for Reaffirm – make sure you have understood all the candidate's answers to your questions

S for Silence – give a candidate a chance to think and reply when you have asked a question – don't feel you have to fill the silence.

Start the interview with **open questions** – using words like "Tell me a bit..." or words like 'How' or 'Why' which give the candidate confidence because these kind of questions give them the opportunity to answer in the way they want.

Later you can start using **closed questions** (eg questions starting with 'What' or 'When') when you may need specific information and clarification of your understanding of what the candidate has said.

Towards the end of the interview you may also wish to ask **more demanding questions** like "Tell me about a time you dealt with an angry or complaining client" or "Describe an unusual work experience and how you coped with it" or "Give an example of outstanding service you have given".

Always give candidates an **opportunity to ask questions**. These questions are often revealing. Answer them fully and honestly.

Remember, **you are being interviewed** as well as the candidate. You have to be considerate, thoughtful and someone the candidate really wants to work with. If you're not, the best candidate may decide your care home is not the right place for her.

End the interview in a positive way explaining to the candidate what you will do, when they will hear the outcome and thanking them for attending.

After the interview

Decide on the candidate you wish to employ. Sometimes it makes sense to ask for a further interview just to be sure. Make sure you follow up any **references** given and they are accurate and satisfactory. Employers are becoming wary of giving opinions about previous employees (in case they get sued) so do not expect a lot in writing but sometimes they are more forthcoming on the telephone.

Once you are sure, **make an enthusiastic offer** so that the candidate feels delighted and thrilled to be joining you. It should be a win-win situation with both parties feeling equally pleased.

Once the candidate has accepted the post make sure **they sign their contract** which sets out the terms and conditions of the post.
Follow up every candidate regardless of whether they have been successful or not. This is common courtesy but it is also good sense because you do not want them complaining about your organisation and how badly you have treated them. The care home world can be quite a small place.

Do not make a job offer because you are desperate to fill a post and it is convenient in the short term. If you know no one you have interviewed is suitable for the job, you will have to restart the whole process again, but it will be shorter and less trouble for you in the long run.

Review your whole interviewing process and decide whether it could be improved. Sorry – not *whether* it could be improved – no one is perfect – rather, *how* it could be improved.

10 questions you might like to use in your interviews

1. What attracted you to our organisation?
2. What kind of work do you most enjoy?
3. What values do you most admire in other people?
4. What experience and qualities can you bring to the role you are interviewing for?
5. What has been your biggest work challenge so far, and what did you learn from it?
6. What are your strengths?
7. What are your weaknesses? (Not a suitable question for all candidates so think carefully before using it)
8. Where would you like to be in your career five years from now?
9. Walk me through a work project which you are particularly proud of
10. Before we close is there anything you would like to tell me which you have not had a chance to say so far?

Retaining staff

Your big challenge

As described above **staff churn** is one of the care manager's biggest challenges. Take a moment to work out the real value of each and every one of your employees. Think hard and don't underestimate how much they do in the home, their years of experience, expertise and personal relationships with the home's clients. Think too about the cost of re-recruiting (including advertising, agency fees, screening, interviewing, training and the paper trail). There is research which suggests that it costs one and a half times the salary of a departing employee to replace them and over half a year before they are performing at their best. And of course on top of the cost you have to add the precious time you and your team spend in the process.

It won't take you long to decide that, as a compassionate and commercially aware manager, better staff retention is a much better option than constantly interviewing possible replacements. You need to retain your good staff. How do you do it?

The key to successful staff retention is to **think of it as a 24-hour, 365 days a year job**. It is tempting when fully staffed to whisper a sigh of relief and turn to one of your other urgent tasks. Big mistake! At this precise moment a percentage of your better staff will be wondering whether to leave and you need to stop them.

You need to be walking the floor of the home, constantly convincing staff that your home – their home – is the best place to be working. You may not be able to pay the best wages but research shows that the best people stay for non-monetary reasons like, for example, being respected and valued. They also want to work in a place which delivers something worthwhile – high quality care in the company of high quality people. Don't linger in your office writing reports on how excellent staff morale is – get out there, be a role model and leader. Prove it to the people who matter: the staff themselves.

Watch for the tell-tale signs of a member of staff member about to leave – a sudden increase in days taken off due to illness for no apparent reason could be because they are interviewing elsewhere. Lateness for work, poor quality work, a new, disinterested look, a lack of enthusiasm for new ideas or projects are all suspicious signs. Ask suspects in for a 'chat' and tell them how much you value them, emphasising all the positives and telling them about some training or new initiative you have been planning for them. When it comes to retaining your best staff you need to be imaginative.

Tell staff how valuable they are and in return make sure they understand all the benefits they are getting from your organisation. The key is to communicate these benefits well. When compared to the costs of recruiting and replacing employees, employee benefits can save you money and time. According to Capita, 34% of employees think that being thanked or receiving recognition is more important than training, promotion or flexi-hours. And one of the most cost effective ways of showing you value your employees is to persuade your senior managers to put in place a package of benefits which employees understand and which actually means something to them in terms of understanding they are valued.

Reward your staff regularly. Small gifts are fine – for the employee of the month for example. It's the act of showing staff that you value them which is what is appreciated.

Offer support to nurses and professional staff with revalidation. Staying compliant can be a big headache and so your help minimizing stress will be very much appreciated.

Outline career pathways and training opportunities for staff. Show all staff that you are committed to helping them become the best in whatever area they choose. Funding appropriate training can be a serious up-front cost but have courage and confidence and it always pays its way in the long run.

Keep recruiting 24 hours a day even if you have – at this moment – all the staff you need. Keep CVs of good staff you may have interviewed but not been able to give a job – an opening may appear for them. Train younger staff so they are ready to step up should a more senior post come up. When attending events keep your eye out for promising people who might be perfect for that job in your home which might come up soon. Visit local colleges, encouraging young people to think of social care as a possible career option. If you don't work and think hard about recruitment while your home is constantly short of staff, even your most loyal staff will become exhausted and stressed and in time leave you.

Make staff proud:

- **Of their home** so they actively want to work there rather than just seeing it as a way to put food on the table
- **Of the quality of care** they give to residents, Individual staff reviews offer the opportunity for you both to think about successes as well as well as things which the individual must improve. Champions will often change their technique when winning as well as when losing if they think it will improve their performance
- **Of themselves** for working there. Staff meetings are a great time to share the care home's successes and – not to be forgotten- those of individuals who have done well. The office is the place to share failures, problems and discussions about required improvements. The purpose is to develop a supportive culture not one of fear.

Making change happen

To be a compassionate and commercially aware manager you are almost certainly going to have to implement change. How best do you go about making change happen?

- **Define what the change** is that you wish to make.
- **Think about why people resist change.** Next think about who will be the people affected and how they will be affected by the proposed change(s). Identify their differing emotional and behavioural responses to the proposals.
- **Use Koller's 8 steps** to making change happen successfully:

1. **Create a sense of urgency** (and excitement) that the change(s) must happen quickly
2. **Build a group of people with power and energy** who are committed to the change(s). Every leader, however good, benefits from help
3. **Create a vision** to help guide the change(s) and develop understandable ways in which the vision can be achieved. Emphasise the importance of a shared vision
4. **Enlist a volunteer army** wanting and willing to make the changes
5. **Identify and remove any threats** and barriers to the change(s)
6. **Make sure there are well-publicised short-term wins** along the way to keep spirits up
7. **Keep the momentum going** by adding new people, ideas and projects
8. **Put the change(s) into action.**

- **Make sure the change(s) is/are embedded** into the 'culture' of the organisation so that it/they cannot be easily replaced or forgotten.

> *People will forget what you said, people will forget what you did, but people will never forget how you made them feel."*
> ***– Maya Angelou, American poet***

The big message: good staff are more valuable than gold

On average **almost 60% of a care home's total costs are taken up by staff wages** (Knight Frank Care Homes Review 2016), easily the biggest single cost for a home. This figure tells you how important staff are and where you need to be putting your time and energy.

Average staff costs per year per resident will vary according to the type of care home and region. In broad outline the most expensive are in the South East (£24,938 per year per resident), South West (£24,390) and London (£24,358). The lowest costs per year are in the North East (£17,355), Yorkshire and The Humber (£18,068) and the North West (£18,701) (Knight Frank Care Homes Review 2016). It should be noted that these costs were compiled before the implementation of the National Living Wage which added 7.5% to lower paid staff wages.

A stable, loyal, well trained workforce is essential for a home to be successful, and one way to achieve this is to **reduce your reliance on agency staff**. Agency staff are valuable, valued people with a very important role rescuing you from emergency staff shortages. They should not be needed to fill regular posts and, if they are, you will need to change this.

How much your home relies on agency staff is one of the most important **key performance indicators (KPIs)** used by senior management to judge how well a home is doing. There are extra wage and non-wage costs in employing GOOD permanent staff but the benefits usually outweigh these, over time: for the following reasons:

- Higher resident satisfaction with familiar and knowledgeable staff
- Reduced time organising recruitment and interviewing once your workforce is stable
- Reduced legal and reputational risks once your staff is engaged and loyal.

If you can **get your agency fees under 7.5%** of your total staff wage bill, the national average, you will be doing very well. **There's your challenge**!

Story: a warning to all

Despite an 'Outstanding' rating, Silk Healthcare was obliged to close its Reuben Manor care home in Yarm, north-east England because of a shortage of trained nurses. Their MD said: "Staffing remains the most important factor in the delivery of our high quality care, and we are not prepared to compromise on the level of dedicated care we give"."

Self-directed reflection

From what you have learnt in this chapter, write below at least five must-do points which you are going to action immediately – yes, immediately!

Notes

The Carrot and Stick: Regulation

What is the purpose of a regulator like CQC inspecting care homes?

Describe five really important things to do when preparing for an inspection from a regulator like CQC.

In Section 9 we will discuss:

- **Inspections are really important**
- **The UK regulators**
- **The regulator's role**
- **Ratings**
- **Enforcement powers**
- **Making sure your inspections are a success: preparation**
- **Making sure your inspections are a success: on the day**
- **Making sure your inspections are a success: afterwards**

Inspections are really important

An inspection from a regulator like CQC is one of the key events in the life of your home. The result could affect the future of your home, certainly its reputation with possible residents, commissioners and all your stakeholders.

Get a good result: heart-warming success for all the team. Yay! Crack out the prosecco!

Get a poor result: things will look rather different. Here's how:

- **Take one of your most interested stake-holders – your bank,** for example. If it has lent your company money there will undoubtedly be a covenant (promise) between the registered care provider of your care home and the bank (the funder) that the provider will report to the funder any serious matters which are, or could be, damaging the care home. A CQC assessment that your care home 'Requires Improvement' or, worse, is 'Inadequate' would definitely be such an event. It could result in the funder 'calling in' the loan (demanding repayment in full) which is something few companies can survive.
- **Follow-up inspections** – always nervous occasions.
- **A real struggle to maintain occupancy,** perhaps due to a local authority embargo on taking new residents, even referrals as well
- **Your line manager/owner coming down on you like a ton of bricks**, possibly worst of all – a commercial meltdown and closure.
- **Even your own career could be at stake** if you can't turn things around.
- **Let's be blunt.** It is impossible to run a commercially successful home if your CQC inspections are a disaster. So... no pressure then! Let's get you prepared.

Your country's regulator

England

The **Care Quality Commission (CQC)** is the non-departmental, regulatory body (like Ofsted for nurseries and schools) which inspects and regulates health and social care settings, including care homes, hospitals, GP and dental practices in England. It was set up in 2009 and drew together three previous organisations:

- The Healthcare Commission
- The Commission for Social Care Inspection (CSCI)
- The Mental Health Act Commission (MHAC).

Scotland

The regulatory body for care homes in Scotland is the **Care Inspectorate** (**CI**) (formally known as Social Care and Social Work Improvement Scotland). It was set up in 2011 by the Scottish Government as a single regulatory body for social work and social care work services including children's services. The new organisation took on work in these areas previously carried out by:

- Her Majesty's Inspectorate of Education (HMIE)
- The Social Work Inspection Agency (SWIA)
- The Care Commission.

Wales

The care home regulator for Wales was established by the Welsh Assembly. **The Care and Social Services Inspectorate Wales (CSSIW)** is the successor body to Care Standards Inspectorate Wales (CSIW) and was established in 2007 when CSIW was merged with the Social Services Inspectorate Wales.

Northern Ireland

In Northern Ireland the regulator for care homes is the **Regulation and Quality Improvement Authority (RQIA).** It was set up by the Northern Ireland Government in 2003 by the Health and Personal Social Services (Quality, Improvement and Regulation) (Northern Ireland) Order as an independent body. The RQIA is responsible for the regulation (which includes registration and inspection) of establishments and agencies delivering health and social care services including children's homes, day care settings, independent clinics, independent hospitals and independent medical agencies, nursing homes, nursing agencies, residential care homes, voluntary adoption agencies, residential family centres and domiciliary care agencies. Under the Order, the RQIA is also responsible for keeping the Government informed about the overall state and provision of services as well as their availability and quality, and for encouraging improvement in the quality of those services by conducting reviews.

The regulator's role

The aims of each of these regulators for people who use regulated services are to:

- Receive applications for the registration of regulated services and to approve those applications which fulfil the registration criteria
- For those services which are approved, to inspect them using the specific regulations which apply to them. Care homes have different regulations to meet compared to, say, hospitals.

In fulfilling its role, the relevant regulator (eg CQC, CI, CSSIW or RQIA) aims to:

- Protect relevant people from harm and the risk of harm – in the case of a care home, the people to be protected are the residents
- Ensure that residents receive appropriate, effective and good-quality care
- Encourage care providers to improve
- Hold care providers and individuals, particularly registered managers, to account for any serious failures in how their service is provided.

The regulator achieves these aims by registering all new care services, regularly inspecting existing services and monitoring a range of data sources that may warn them about potential problems with provider services (eg financial information for big providers so the regulator is pre-warned in case one of these companies goes into administration resulting in a lot of homes being obliged to close).

Paul Gilbert

Paul Gilbert, FBPsS, PhD, OBE is Professor of Clinical Psychology at the University of Derby and Consultant Clinical Psychologist at the Derbyshire Health Care Foundation Trust. He is also a well-known researcher, speaker and trainer. Paul founded The Compassionate Mind Foundation in 2006. The foundation supports global academic research and created the Annual Global Conference on Compassion by bringing leaders in this field together. The Compassionate Mind Foundation's work is based on Paul's research over his career which has been a focus on shame and the treatment of shame based difficulties, which is where Compassion Focused Therapy (CFT) was established. The foundation now practices and promotes CFT which is used by thousands of clinicians around the world.

This manual's role

For the sake of simplicity and the avoidance of repetition **this manual will be referring to the practice of CQC** when it comes to regulatory matters. In broad principle all regulators work in line with this practice so wherever in the UK you work the advice given in this manual will be valuable. However, there are undoubtedly differences between each of the four nation's regulators, some quite significant. So, **to be an effective compassionate and commercially aware manager you will need to get to know your particular regulator well. Indeed, sometimes you will need to go further and try to understand the individual interpretation of regulations by your particular inspector.**

Every regulatory body claims it tries to make every inspection 'a level playing field' but in *Caring Times'* experience this goal has never been achieved and is unlikely to be so until robots replace the fallible human. **We cannot emphasise enough, therefore, how important it is for the manager to remain flexible, adaptable, well-organised, communicative and aware at all times during the inspection process.**

A Government report (*Cutting Red Tape*) showed that the average home spent 16 days per year dealing with inspections (not just CQC ones – local authority inspections too) and 25 days per year collecting and collating data for them. This is already a long time away from a manager's main purpose which is providing the required leadership needed to deliver outstanding care for their residents. **So you definitely do not want to be wasting unnecessary extra time because you are disorganised.**

Ratings

The four ratings introduced (2014) by CQC
Your inspector will give your home one of these four ratings:

Outstanding

The service is performing exceptionally well.
Brilliant outcome. Well done. You probably don't need to read this section and perhaps even the whole manual! Don't get complacent though – remember there is only one direction to go ratings-wise.

Good

The service is performing well and meeting CQC's expectations.
Good work. Well done. There are plenty of fine services which are only interested in consistent 'Goods' so you should be proud of yourself. But there is still... 'Outstanding' to strive for.

Requires improvement

The service isn't performing as well as it should and CQC has told the service what areas must improve.
Don't panic. There are plenty of other 'Requires Improvement' ratings being issued – low hundreds per month. But this is an action call – big time – and you need to respond immediately or some of the serious CQC enforcement powers described below will start to be used.

Inadequate

The inspector has concluded that the service is performing badly and CQC has taken action against the person or organisation that runs it.
Just under 10% of homes are getting this rating. If yours is one of them your home is in big trouble and you and your line manager/owner and your entire team are going to have to work exceptionally hard to 'save' the home. Otherwise it may be closed and your residents will be forced to move – something they rightly hate to do, and your staff will be made redundant and your management career will certainly stutter if not grind to a halt.

CQC has key concerns which you have to think about because they are the ones most likely to result in this 'Inadequate' rating. The two most important are:

- The safety of residents
- The quality of leadership.

What is a warning notice?

A Warning Notice describes:

- The regulations which CQC claims your home is not meeting
- The evidence the inspector is relying upon in reaching the conclusion that a given regulation is not being met.

The Warning Notice will specify how much time CQC will allow you to achieve compliance.

The Warning Notice will also say what will happen should your home fail to comply with the given regulation(s). In this case CQC:

- May take further action that might include cancellation of the registration of the care service and/or the cancellation of your registration as 'registered manager'. Both actions would be very serious for the care provider and your future career in management of a care service.
- May publish the actions it has taken more widely. That action will probably include informing:
  - all local authorities with whom the care service is contracted; and
  - the press and media.

Of course, you are given an opportunity to respond to the regulator, but only have 10 days to do so. There is no route to appeal a Warning Notice.

Enforcement powers

CQC has both civil and criminal powers.

If your home receives either a 'Requires improvement' or 'Inadequate' rating, CQC will use an escalating approach, depending on severity, to using its enforcement powers:

1. **Requiring improvement:** CQC will use its civil powers to issue either requirement or warning notices.

2. **Forcing improvement:** CQC can **enforce standards** by using its civil powers to impose, vary or remove conditions of registration including:
   - Suspending a registration
   - Cancelling a registration.

   CQC can use a time-limited approach, in combination with other oversight bodies, to ensure your home's inadequate care is not allowed to continue. These are:
   - Use urgent procedures
   - Impose special measures.

3. **Holding providers and individuals to account for failures utilising criminal powers.** Care providers, directors and employees can now face criminal charges for offences such as ill-treatment, wilful neglect, gross negligence manslaughter and corporate manslaughter. Failure to comply with conditions of registration or to continue to provide a regulated activity after suspension or cancellation of registration are also criminal offences. **In a nutshell – CQC is now the lead inspector and enforcer for safety and quality of care for care home providers.** However, if there is a suspicion of ill-treatment or wilful neglect this will probably fall to **the police** to investigate and, if there is sufficient evidence to justify prosecution, those said to have committed these crimes will find themselves summoned to attend the criminal courts.

There are six significant pieces of legislation which you should be aware of. Hopefully you will not meet them in the ordinary course of your professional life and it will only be enthusiasm and professional curiosity which makes you look them up rather than more pressing, legal reasons!

1. Prosecutions under the Health and Safety at Work etc Act (1974) are now becoming increasingly common.
2. All investigations into criminal offences are carried out with reference to the Police and Criminal Evidence Act (1984) ('PACE').
3. The Health & Social Care Act 2008 (Regulated Activities) Regulations (2014) marked the most significant recent increase in powers for CQC as it took on criminal powers previously used by the Health and Safety Executive (HSE) for health & safety matters.
4. The Criminal Justice and Courts Act (2015) saw the introduction of new offences of ill-treatment and wilful neglect and the extension of these offences to care providers and directors as well a care workers.
5. The implementation of the Health and Safety Offences, Corporate Manslaughter and Food Hygiene Offences Definitive Sentencing Guideline in 2016 provided sentencing guidelines for all organisations and individuals (aged 18 and over) dependent on how blameworthy the defendant was (four grades – very high, high, medium and low), the harm caused and the size of the organisation (the bigger the organisation, the bigger the fine).
6. The Mental Capacity Act 2005 (Sect 44) created the criminal offences of ill-treatment and wilful neglect of a person lacking mental capacity.

In addition, a **Memorandum of Understanding (MoU) in 2015 in England between CQC, the Health and Safety Executive and local authorities** effectively passed to CQC the lead for investigating and prosecuting CQC-registered health and adult social care providers where a service user is affected by a failure of the provider to provide safe care and/or treatment.

Can you/your organisation challenge CQC?

The answer is definitely **'Yes'** but you may well need expert legal advice and help in formulating any response to CQC and the sooner the better. What options are there?

1. **Do nothing:** Very careful consideration will need to be given to all the relevant factors before 'sitting back and doing nothing', especially if the inspector is wrong in fact or in law.

2. **Representations:** Written representations can be made about certain types of enforcement action including the following:
   - Warning notices
   - Notice of proposal to impose, vary or remove a condition of registration
   - Notice of proposal to suspend a registration
   - Notice of proposal to cancel a registration.

   Is there a time limit for making representations?
   Yes. Section 27(1) of the Health and Social Care Act 2008 says that representations must be made within '28 days of service of the Notice' by CQC. CQC should respond within 20 days but this is not legally binding.
   In relation to representations in response to a Warning Notice, CQC requires a response within 10 working days.

   The best place to find detailed guidance about representations is the CQC themselves – well done CQC! However, to be completely sure about time limits, you ought to look at the specified regulations themselves.

Story

The first corporate manslaughter conviction of a care home provider took place at the end of 2015 following the death of an 86-year-old resident. Sherwood Rise Ltd was fined £300,000. In addition the director in day-to-day charge of the home was sentenced to three years and two months in prison for gross negligence manslaughter and the care home manager was awarded one year in prison, suspended for two years for breaches of the Health and Safety at Work Act (1974).

3. **Appeals: appeals can be made against:**
   - A notice of decision
   - A notice of imposed, varied or removed conditions using urgent procedures
   - A court order to cancel a registration using urgent procedures.

Registered persons have the right to appeal to the First-tier Tribunal (Care Standards) against enforcement action using CQC's civil enforcement procedures. This includes action under urgent procedures which can be fast tracked.

However, remember there is no route to appeal a Warning Notice.

Is there a time limit for making appeals?
Yes. Appeals have to be made within 28 days of the receipt of the CQC Notice of Decision.

How to make an appeal

You can find out more about appealing against Notices of Decision on the First-tier Tribunal Service's website. Then follow the links to the First-tier Tribunal (Care Standards).

www.gov.uk/government/organisations/hm-courtsand-tribunals-service/about

Three letters to remember: CQC

Remember to use CQC's own three letters to remind yourself how to (and how not to) work with them best:

Make certain you are:	Make certain you are definitely not:
Communicative	**C**areless
Quick	**Q**uarrelsome
Co-operative	**C**lueless

Embargoes: Legal Tips

From time-to-time, either a local authority and/or CQC may have serious concerns about aspects of a care home service. This might include the home being placed in CQC special measures, safeguarding or abuse issues or serious financial issues like the home going into administration. They will seek to prevent (embargo) a care provider from accepting new residents into their care home. Often, one or other will ask the management to agree to a 'voluntary' embargo – but if there is no agreement they will seek to impose one.

The legal position with respect to the local authority is that it should have reserved the power, by the contract it has with the home, to suspend placements of people in the care home and even to cease making referrals to you. However, get the contract out, dust it off, and read it to establish whether 'your' local authority has done so. If not, it can't impose an embargo. It can, however, serve notice to terminate the contract with you.

CQC is in a slightly different position. In essence it has no legal power to directly impose an embargo. Rather, if it does not secure your voluntary agreement, it may seek to impose a condition of registration on the care home preventing further admissions of new residents– a process which is rather longer to impose and rather more difficult.

As mentioned above, you will probably be asked to voluntarily agree to an embargo. It might well be best to agree so that you can keep a measure of control over the situation. The way to do so is to agree to an embargo in writing (drafted by you, or better still, by your lawyer) in which you reserve for yourself the power to terminate the embargo on seven days' written notice. You must then do all in your power to solve the problems causing the embargo so that it can be lifted.

Making sure your inspections are a success: preparation

Be prepared and confident

If you are well prepared, you will feel confident.

☐ **Go to the CQC website (www.cqc.org)** and read every word (several times) so you know exactly what you are being judged against. Inspectors will use standard key lines of enquiry (KLOEs – find them in the Appendices to CQC's *Residential Adult Social Care Provider Handbook)* directly related to the five key areas CQC will be focusing on:

1. Are you running a safe care setting?
Yes. Your customers and staff are protected from abuse, neglect and avoidable harm.

2. Are you effective?
Yes. Your care, treatment and support for residents meets their individual needs, helps them to maintain a good quality of life and is supported by research. Your thorough care plans show how good your care is.

3. Are you caring?
Yes. Your staff involve and treat residents with compassion, kindness, dignity and respect. They have enough time to sit with – and reassure – any distressed or unsettled residents. They are able to spend good quality time with residents, not just when a task needs doing. Spending time with residents like this is important but can be hard to do when budgets are under pressure. However, outstanding care homes manage to achieve it.

4. Are you responsive to people's needs?
Yes. Your services are organised so that they meet residents' needs. One way of knowing is **carrying out surveys** of your residents, their relatives, and your staff. The surveys can either be general, or focus on one topic like meals and mealtimes or entertainment or activities. Your Care Rating is an independent and well respected survey of residents and relatives which you may wish to consider.

www.yourcarerating.org

Having conducted a survey, though, **you must, must, must review** the replies, write a plan to meet any issues found and put it into action. Without this review, plan and action, the surveys are pretty pointless and CQC will criticise you – and rightly so!

5. Is the service well-led?
Yes. The management of your organisation and care service are experienced and motivated to provide exceptional care for their residents. They make sure that their service:

- Is providing high-quality care, including care plans, which is based around every resident's individual needs.
- Encourages staff to learn and experience. ☐ Staff supervision details, ☐ disciplinary records and ☐ appraisals should be reviewed in case they are requested.
- Promotes a supportive but also challenging culture which is willing to try new ideas.
- Promotes an open, diverse, equal and fair culture for all.
- Works in partnership with individuals and groups outside the home to improve the service and provide a valuable community service.
- Regularly reviews ☐ management,

Improve your preparation for an inspection

Five suggestions on how to improve your preparation for a CQC inspection – in case you want to add to your own answers to the first question in this section:

1. **Review resident care plans** – plug any gaps which exist, and ensure that they are up to date. For example, if a resident has had a fall, make sure that there was a falls assessment and that any necessary actions identified have taken place.
2. **Make sure that there are well recorded Mental Capacity Act assessments.**
3. **Make sure your audit medication records are up to date.**
4. **Make sure your audit training records are up to date.**
5. **Make sure that residents' and relatives' surveys have been reviewed**, that records of the reviews exist and any action points have actually been 'actioned' or there is a plan to do so.

And one for luck! Review your accidents and incidents file to be sure that all relevant notifications have been made to the appropriate bodies. Rookie error if they haven't and one which gives inspectors totally the wrong impression and they will rightly jump all over you.

☐ governance, ☐ leadership and ☐ audit systems to ensure they are up to date and effective.

☐ **Work with your line manager to make sure that you have an effective quality management system (QMS) in place**. Using an all-year-round continual programme of auditing will help you and your team achieve the requirements and outcomes you need. It will also give your inspector confidence that your home is well-run and uses modern technology and methods.

Make sure that all activity/improvements made are recorded. Even if you have simply had a review and no action has been found to be necessary, make a note of that fact and sign and date the record.

☐ **No excuses... you have to keep up to date.** You can't allow essentials such as policy reviews, staff records or risk assessments to get out of date or forgotten.

If your QMS doesn't have one, make a schedule at the beginning of the year for all your policies that will need reviewing/renewing. A simple spreadsheet will allow you to code all your policies and then – to make sure you are putting them into practice – answer **five questions for each policy review**:

☐ **What** – precisely - is the policy review work that needs to be done?
☐ **Who** is going to do the review work?
☐ **When** are the deadlines which need to be met?
☐ **How** will the review work be done?
☐ **Where** will the review work be done?

Important: Remember a policy review does not necessarily mean that a policy must be amended or rewritten. Simply reading the document and satisfying oneself that no further action is needed is perfectly acceptable. However, there must be a written record that the policy was read, reviewed and accepted.

Keep your staff training up to date because this is something all CQC inspectors will be looking for. Some ideas include:

- Keeping a 'training passport' for every staff member which holds details of any statutory or mandatory training that they need to do alongside their personal development objectives from their annual appraisal can be very helpful.
- Encourage every member of the team to understand that keeping up to date

> *The golden principle for any good society is to do unto others as you would they do unto you.*
> *– The Golden Rule described in many religions and cultures*

is partly their responsibility.

- Keep a spreadsheet of all training needs for each member of staff and record training / retraining / new training on the spreadsheet.

☐ **Doing well in inspections is not a one-person job** – it needs everyone in the care home, from 'hotel' and client services, to the maintenance person, the housekeeper, the kitchen staff as well as you and your care staff to take responsibility to be prepared and perform on the day:

- **Organise practice inspections** so all staff, residents and relatives know what to expect from inspections and therefore behave confidently. Perhaps another experienced manager in your organisation could take you through the process and suggest improvements. Staff will find the experience of answering real questions really helpful. Staff often say they feel intimidated by the inspection process, so the more practice they can have the easier it becomes. It's true for you too.
- **Make sure staff have got used to being watched** by people (inspectors) while at work. Nothing is worse than staff hiding away during an inspection leaving residents unattended as well as communal areas looking empty and neglected. Again, practice helps.
- **Make sure there is always someone responsible at the home** who is briefed to be in charge of an inspection should one occur when you are away.
- **Encourage staff** to understand that their all-important training – which CQC rightly values greatly – is as much their responsibility as yours. Better participation and attendance will be the result and the inspector will notice.

☐ **Anticipate what is likely to happen during the inspection so that you are well prepared:**

- **Take a tour of your home as if you were the inspector. Make notes of this 'mock inspection':**
  1. **You need to look at the premises with fresh eyes**, starting at the front gate and visiting every part of the home, asking questions all the time. Perhaps take the team responsible for maintenance with you. Have you got too used to the shabby paint, leaking gutters or toilets which sometimes smell, for example? Is the reception too full of notices and warnings to give the welcoming feel you want? There will be lots you have to think about. Have a checklist which you tick off and add to as you go round.
  2. **Look closely at your residents**. Are they looking well cared for (make sure that any food/drink spillages on clothes are addressed promptly by staff)? Do they look happy? Do they look engaged and animated? Are they interacting with staff and other residents? What activities are available for them? Are relatives clearly involved? Another checklist needed.
  3. **Look closely at your staff**. Do they look relaxed and confident? Do they look as if they have been well trained? Do they knock on doors before entering rooms? Do they obtain consent from residents before carrying out tasks? Are they interacting appropriately with residents and colleagues? Are they familiar with CQC language and thinking including areas such as equality and diversity, risk assessments and human rights?

- Review the notes from the 'mock inspection' and **put into action what needs to be done**.

- **Find the home's previous inspection** and read the report. You may find reported weaknesses which the inspector will focus on, and you need to be ready for them.
- **Think ahead about the popular areas** which you can expect your inspector to concentrate on: ☐ care planning, ☐ infection control, ☐ medication, ☐ safeguarding, ☐ health and safety, ☐ auditing of accidents, ☐ external areas, ☐ activities, ☐ training, ☐ recruitment, ☐ interviewing technique, ☐ staff induction and ☐ appropriate supervision are just some areas for you to think about.
- **Keep a tidy office** so you and your staff know where to find everything. Care plans (easily lost) must be available (and fully completed) for every resident. ☐ Training spreadsheets, ☐ staffing rosters, ☐ property maintenance checks, ☐ staff training details, ☐ all the annual checks like fire and equipment must be available.
- **Make a good show.** During an inspection some managers display prominently on their desk a copy of the Regulations or CQC's '*Guidance for providers on meeting the regulations*' which helpfully sets out each of the regulations separately and then, beneath each, provides CQC guidance on the particular regulation. There might also be, on a nearby shelf, copies of the eight provider handbooks. All of this can make a good show which can impress the inspector, especially if the documents look as if they are well read (a few coffee stains can help!). Ultimately, though, the important point is that you are very familiar with the regulations and make their enforcement part of your daily activity as manager of the service.

> *Compassion is when you care enough to help someone with their problem and take time to find out what's bothering 'em.*
> *– Fidgel, 321 Penguins*

www.cqc.org.uk/sites/default/files/20150324_guidance_providers_meeting_regulations_01.pdf

- **Think ahead if you know your care home has failings** and make sure that your inspector knows you already have a plan to solve them. Nasty, unexpected shocks are not good for anybody – especially not for your inspector or for you.

Making sure your inspections are a success: on the day

First – don't panic!

On the whole CQC inspectors are normal people who just want to do their job well and reward good care when they find it. This fact was acknowledged by Andrea Sutcliffe, the CQC's Chief Inspector of Adult Social Care, in an article in *Caring Times* where she said: "*Day in, day out, my inspection teams see examples of people experiencing great care as a result of fantastic managers and staff who are supported by strong leadership. Together they promote a culture of listening and acting on the voices of people, and their families, using services – and above all – do not cut corners when it comes to quality of care.*"

Of course there are exceptions but what you definitely don't want to do by your behaviour or attitude is turn a reasonable inspector into one who is determined to 'mark you down'.

The key is to feel genuinely confident about the quality of your home. That confidence your

The carrot and stick

The '**carrot and stick**' approach describes a policy of offering a combination of **rewards** and **punishment** to influence behaviour. It refers to the practice of cart drivers who sometimes dangle a carrot in front of a mule and also hold a stick behind it. The mule is inclined to move forwards towards the carrot because it wants the reward of food, while also moving forwards to avoid the punishment of pain from the stick behind it. The combined effect of the carrot and the stick achieves what the driver wants – to move the cart forwards.

home will perform well whenever it is inspected will be felt by all your staff, your residents and relatives, and most importantly, your inspector:

- **Be friendly and flexible** to fit in with the inspector's plans/routine. Some managers like to show the inspector around the care home themselves, others think it puts less pressure on everyone including the inspector if someone less senior does this. Whoever does it must know the home inside out and especially residents' personal histories so they can start conversations with residents (and relatives) and their co-workers as the inspection progresses.
- **Be friendly and supportive to the expert by experience** who will be informally 'interviewing' residents, relatives and other visitors. They will have agreed some questions with the inspector in advance which will be based around the 'safe, effective, caring, responsive and well led' concept and will be wanting to get them answered for their report. One question they often ask residents and relatives is "How do you spend your day?" Many experts like to hear that residents are involved in activities of daily living (like cleaning or dusting) or are taking an active role in the running of the home in the kitchen or garden for example.
- **Don't become anxious** if the inspector has clearly done some information gathering on your home before visiting – which will invariably be the case. It simply means they are doing their job well and are less likely to make an instant and unfair judgement.

The staff team need to perform well on the day. Some of the key things that they need to know about will include:

- ☐ **Where all your policies and protocols are kept** and the content of those which are relevant to their job in the care home.
- ☐ **The information provided for residents and relatives** about the services available and all the ways in which they can be accessed.
- ☐ Your staff need to **recognise that the 'little things' that they do** for individual residents, relatives and co-workers will be taken as important evidence by CQC inspectors for several of the CQC standards. Staff members may think that they are just 'doing their job', but examples of the ways in which they meet the needs of individual patients is powerful evidence of good practice.
- ☐ **Staff need to be warned to be careful about how they answer leading questions** from inspectors like 'Do you think more staff would be helpful?' If they answer 'Yes' as would seem to be reasonable in even well-staffed homes, the CQC report may come back reporting that 'a member of staff told us there were not enough staff'.
- ☐ Staff need to understand that CQC inspectors are very keen to **see that residents and their loved ones have opportunities to give feedback**, and that the team listens to it and acts upon it where appropriate. For example, if you have a customer participation or liaison

group, make sure that your staff can describe ways in which the feedback has been acted upon. Resident and relative meetings should be minuted and those minutes kept and reviewed from time to time to make sure that sensible improvements are continually occurring. Regular 'tweaks' to how and when things are done are helpful in showing that yours is a listening and learning service. Make sure these tweaks are recorded.

- ☐ Encourage your staff to take a look at the profiles section on the **CQC website** where **reports of other inspections** can be found. There is a lot to be learnt there and it might be worth discussing the findings at your team meetings. Make it part of their training. Revisit it, say, annually.
- ☐ Most importantly, **give your staff total confidence that your residents are safe** within the home. If staff are confident that the care each resident receives meets their needs and all the latest standards and guidance then they are much more likely to convince the inspector of the same thing.

The person accompanying the inspector should take notes about:

- ☐ Where the inspector went
- ☐ Who the inspector met
- ☐ What happened of note during the inspection
- ☐ What was said of note either by the inspector or a member of staff, resident or relative.

Hopefully there will be no need to challenge what happened at the inspection but should this be necessary, accurate notes will make the difference between success and failure.

Beware: protect yourself

This manual is primarily about helping managers to understand commercial matters better so that they can provide outstanding and compassionate care. However it would be irresponsible for us not to draw your attention to the increased risk of potential prosecution by the police, Health & Safety Executive and CQC since new sentencing guidelines came into force in February 2016. Fines and prison sentences have already increased. Managers should note the increased frequency by CQC in using its prosecution powers. Examples include:

- A smaller care home company was fined £300,000 for corporate manslaughter of a resident and the home manager was sentenced to 3 years and 2 months imprisonment.
- A large not-for-profit organisation was fined £400,000 when a 91-year old resident died after falling from her bed.
- A medium sized company was fined £1.5 million after a person living with dementia died falling down stairs – and was also ordered to pay costs of £200,000.
- A community services company was prosecuted by CQC and fined £190,000 plus costs after a resident died after falling at one of its care homes.
- A not-for-profit company was fined £50,000 in a prosecution brought by CQC after the death of a resident in one of its care homes.

The last two of these examples demonstrate the increase in activity by CQC in using its prosecution powers. This trend is likely to continue. As manager you are in the firing line when there is the potential for prosecution. As soon as there is any hint that this may happen to you or a member of your staff inform your senior management staff so that you get expert legal advice early. Suspects interviewed under caution under the Police and Criminal Evidence Act have a right to legal representation, and it is clearly important to ensure that appropriately qualified and expert solicitors who understand the care home sector undertake this role. For example, there may also be times where it would be best to refuse to answer questions but instead provide a written statement. If you are a nurse and a member of the Royal College of Nursing you may be entitled to 'free' legal advice from one of its lawyers – consider using that resource.

At the end of an inspection:

- **You should make a point of meeting with the inspector**, and if it is an inspection over several days, then at the end of each day of inspection, to receive formal feedback. If not, ask for it. Make sure that you have someone with you to make a full and careful note of all that is said.
- **If the feedback is highly critical** or contains lots of 'small' criticisms ask the inspector "And what did you find positive about the service?" You need to try to receive some positives from the inspector, and if you are not going to receive those positives you need to be ready when the full negatives arrive later in the post.

Making sure your inspections are a success: afterwards

Work with CQC to make sure you have a factually accurate report post-inspection. If you are happy with the draft report they send you, brilliant. If you are not, you only have 10 working days to consider it and to point out any factual inaccuracies.

- In your submissions try to avoid opinion and instead rely on showing that the CQC evidence presented is inaccurate.
- It can help if you can provide fresh evidence to back up your concerns.
- If you are unhappy with your proposed rating in the draft report, now is the time to address these concerns. If you leave it later than your 10 day deadline, it will be too late. Again, using CQC's factual accuracy process is one of the most successful ways to challenge a proposed rating. If inaccuracies can be proven there is a very good chance that the rating can be improved.
- Getting specialist legal advice at this stage can improve your chances of success.

By dealing promptly and efficiently with any issues raised by the inspector(s) you will give them confidence that you are taking their concerns seriously and are determined to take appropriate action. For example, if you know that an inspector has a particular concern, then it makes sense to address that concern even before the draft report is received – the inspector is bound to be impressed!

Updating CQC with what you are doing – communicating strongly with them all the time – will give them further confidence you are an appropriate person to be caring for vulnerable people, and will help prevent them from taking unwanted enforcement action such as issuing a warning notice.

Story

A care home in North London was given a 'needs improvement' rating. The manager, Carol, noticed that among her comments the inspector had noted that, "There seemed very little communication among the residents and staff." Carol thought about this and realised that a number of the residents the inspector had observed spoke mainly Urdu while none of the staff were able to. Bingo! Carol remembered that one of the Urdu-speaking residents was an ex-teacher so she asked her to lead Urdu classes for some staff volunteers. The teacher was delighted to help and so were all her resident friends! The teacher organised regular Urdu teaching sessions but insisted that most of the learning and practising would be done during ordinary daily activities. In subsequent weeks and months not a lot of Urdu was learnt, it has to be said, but everyone had a lot of fun, joking and teasing, the atmosphere in the home changed wonderfully and next time the inspector came, she awarded the home a satisfying 'Good'. The teaching also counted as a 'meaningful' activity for the resident who was leading it!

Self-directed reflection

Write down 5 things you are going to do now to improve your inspections

Notes

Summary

You have read all the sections, ticked boxes and written down thoughts and action points. Hopefully you are a lot wiser and more knowledgeable than when you started.

But you are not finished yet! Nobody ever finishes learning about how to care better. So – as part of that process – you are not finished with this manual either. There will have been much that you missed first time around and there will be much more besides you will want to think about in greater depth. Here are some key messages from each of the sections to help guide you towards the areas you would most like to revisit:

Section 1

We make no apologies for saying that to achieve your ambitions to be a great and compassionate manager you need to be commercially aware. Understanding commerce and business better is simply a 'means' to your 'end' – which is to run a wonderful, warm home where your residents can live truly happy and self-fulfilled lives.

Section 2

We suggest that to be a successful manager you need to have the right attitude of mind, believing that being commercially aware is important. You need to understand how business and commerce works, both within the wider world and within your own organisation. You need a vision, a strategic plan and the ability to make it all work for your residents, your staff, your local community and your stakeholders. There are various techniques you should become familiar with including the SWOT analysis.

Section 3

An understanding of how businesses are funded and your care home/organisation in particular is helpful because it gives you insight into the pressures funders and owners are under and helps you make good, appropriate decisions at the right time.

Section 4

You don't need to be an accountant to run a care home but you should feel confident about understanding the two most important financial statements, the profit and loss (P&L) account and the balance sheet. There's no need to be anxious – they are not hard to understand and the more you work with them, the more familiar and easy they will become.

Section 5

We help you stay calm about budgeting. Every care home will use budgets and your aim must be to feel totally confident about reading and using them.

Section 6

You need to understand why 'cash is king' is such an important – and true – statement. We help you learn how cash works and its relationship with profit.

Section 7

As a care home manager there is one figure you will think about a lot – your occupancy figure. By great marketing, creating a five ★★★★★ culture, great selling and collecting fees successfully you can make sure this important figure never gives you reasons to worry.

Section 8

One of the biggest challenges facing an organisation is how best to attract the best people and then make the best use of their talents. We show you how organisations set about doing this and how you can contribute by finding, building and keeping the best team.

Section 9

"It is impossible to run a commercially successful home if your CQC inspections are a disaster" is probably the most brutal and blunt statement in the manual. However, by preparing well, doing the right things on the big day and afterwards, you can make sure a regulatory disaster does not strike you.

Extra Info

Commercial analysis tools

The PESTLE Analysis of external factors

The PESTLE analysis is a commonly used and helpful tool which you may wish to use (having mastered the SWOT analysis, page 24) to analyse external factors impacting on your organization in greater depth.

PESTLE stands for

Political
Economic
Social
Technological
Legal
Eco-environmental.

How to carry out a PESTLE analysis

Write down the PESTLE headings on a piece of paper or a board. Next, brainstorm all the possible aspects that could be affecting your industry, organisation or department.

Political could include local, national or even international government actions that affect and influence the way that your care home business operates. The policies may be in favour of or against your sector.

Economic includes factors such as interest rates or taxation or financial support for local authorities or other monetary related items that have an impact on your organisation.

Social factors are trends that make people more or less inclined to buy your services. For example, is there an increasing move towards homecare? If so, is it significant enough to impact on your business, and what can you do to 'ride the wave' and take advantage of your expertise and resources to make the best of the trend? Could you start offering a homecare service yourself?

Technology includes IT that changes the way your organisation operates, for example marketing using sophisticated social media to increase the demand for your services.

Legal developments may mean your organisation needs to change how it operates. For the purpose of your care home you should include also the **regulatory** environment under this heading because your local CQC and local authority decisions are vital to your future.

Environmental issues are important for many sectors but do not seem to have made a big impact in the care home sector so far. If you can focus on some key environmental areas which suit your home (for example how you dispose of your waste products or the fact you grow vegetables for the residents to eat) you may be able to achieve a competitive advantage over rivals.

Carry out a PESTLE analysis of your care home using the table on the next page. Often 'first' thoughts are the most imaginative and innovative.

PESTLE ANALYSIS FOR:	
Political	**Economic**
Social	**Technological**
Legal	**Environmental**

Porter's Five Forces

How competitive are you?

Any business must assess their competitive strength and position. Michael Porter developed the most famous tool – known as **Porter's Five Forces** – for doing so. This tool can be used in combination with other tools such as SWOT and PESTLE.

The five main headings offer a model to develop a broad and sophisticated analysis of your competitive position, as well as helping with forward plans, strategy and investment decisions. They are:

1. Existing competitive rivalry
2. Threat of new market entrants
3. Bargaining power of buyers
4. Power of suppliers
5. Threat of substitute products.

For the care home manager the importance of Porter's Five Forces is:

1. **Existing competitive rivalry.** You need to know what your local competition is offering in terms of facilities, particular areas of expertise, price, staff wages and any special benefits. Much of that information may be on their websites but sometimes you need more. Some consider 'secret shopping' of local homes to be unethical but we think that it is an acceptable practice because it is information gathering rather than being in any way damaging. Whatever your view, it is vital that you know exactly what your competition is doing so that they do not get an edge over you, unknown to you. On the other side of the coin you might consider whether to work with one or more of your 'competitors' on the basis that you are all in the same position and you might as well work together for mutual advantage. For example, sharing training costs across a number of homes can work really well and everyone benefits from having better trained staff. It is usually worth joining your local care home association so you are better informed about local developments and how other homes are responding.

2. **Threat of new market entrants.** New entrants are always a possible threat to a business. When analysing where the likeliest threat is going to come from think 'What? Why? Where? When? How? and Who?' as far as new possibilities are concerned; and what sort of plan you would make if you were in their place. Of course, half the answer to keeping them out is to offer such a great product yourself that there are no opportunities for them.

3. **Bargaining power of buyers.** As far as care homes are concerned buyers are the potential residents and their families. It is vital you know what fees are being charged elsewhere. Knowledge is power here and you should be updating constantly, certainly every six months about your main rivals. It doesn't matter whether you and your team decide to set your fees at a more expensive or cheaper level. The key is that you know exactly why you have chosen your level and are prepared to stick with it until you have good reason to change. The local authority (LA) is the other significant buyer - for clients who are being funded by them. Again you should check that you are being offered the correct fees by the LA for each client, what and whether they have special rates for specialty care (eg dementia) and, as far as possible, what rates they are paying other homes. Sometimes it is possible to meet the buyers at their offices, although be warned that many are reluctant. Sometimes their managers will visit your home and you should view this as a positive opportunity to show your home in its best possible light and to create a relationship if possible – this can be frustrating but be persistent.

4. **Suppliers of goods and services to your home.** If you are the manager of a home belonging to a group, most of the major buying decisions may have been made by head office. Conglomerates which supply a wide range of products needed by homes can be cheaper because of the volumes they supply and their buying power. This apparent cheapness should not be used as an excuse to neglect efforts to keep costs under control. By monitoring costs closely you will make sure you stay under budget and you may be able to give useful feedback back to head office. Sometimes it is possible to make savings by buying locally. For example, seasonal fresh fruit and vegetables will be popular with residents and their families and offer another excellent opportunity to join in with your local community as well as involving clients, your chef and staff in the running of the home. Managers of single homes will have greater flexibility over buying decisions. Make the most of them – take the opportunities to buy locally, for example.

5. **Threat of substitute products (eg technological advances creating the opportunity to replace some of the tasks currently done by humans).** There is no doubt that the increasing sophistication of the technology available to **homecare providers** (particularly being able to monitor clients at home) means that they are now able to care for people with greater dependency and this presents a challenge to care homes. However, such homecare is always going to be limited by its additional costs, by the unpredictable nature of caring for people at home with conditions such as dementia and by ethical issues such as the increasing recognition of the loneliness of older people living at home depending only on short, infrequent visits by care staff.

Assisted living is a new model increasingly on offer in the UK. It appeals to frail people who are not yet ready to go into residential care and has many benefits. One reason it has not gained greater popularity is that it is not a final solution to frailty – relatives in particular fear having to uproot their loved one too often.

VAT

Important note: The fees charged by care homes are VAT exempt so care home companies are generally not registered for VAT. This exemption means much of the information below does not apply to care home fees.

However VAT will be charged by companies providing goods and services to care homes so it is important the care manager understands the general principles of how the tax works.

Value added tax (VAT) is a government tax on the end user (eg ordinary people and businesses) when they buy goods and services in the UK and Europe. It is also known as a goods and services tax (GST), for example in Australia.

Unlike most taxes VAT is collected on behalf of the government by the organisations/ businesses which sell the goods and services (in other words, businesses act as a kind of unpaid tax collector). The tax:

- is calculated by deciding which rate (percentage) of tax applies to the particular good or service supplied
- is added when payment (eg invoices and bills) is first requested
- is calculated on the full cost of the goods or services supplied.

Currently there are three different rates of VAT in the UK:

- **Standard rate:** This rate is currently 20% and is applied on most goods and services in the UK unless otherwise stated. So, if a VAT registered business charges £10 for a service and is applying a standard rate it will add 20% VAT (amounting to £2) and the total bill/ invoice to the end user will rise to £12. The business will keep its £10 and every quarter the £2 VAT will be sent to Her Majesty's Revenue and Customs along with the other VAT collected during the three months by the organisation.
- **Reduced rate:** The reduced rate is 5% and is added, for example, to bills for services such as electricity and gas for people's private homes and for goods such as children's car seats.
- **Zero rate**: This, as the name implies, is 0% and applies to such goods as most foods (but not restaurant meals or takeaways), water and sewage services, children's clothes, books, newspapers and magazine etc.

Any goods/services which do not fall within these three rates (like care home fees for example) are either exempt from VAT or outside the scope of VAT which means VAT should not be charged on them.

In case you are still unsure...

There is an important difference between goods and services which are zero-rated VAT and VAT exempt:

- **Zero-rated VAT:** Even though there is no VAT charged on zero-rated supplies, the zero-rate is still a rate of tax within the VAT system, and businesses that provide zero-rated goods and services can still register for VAT and recover from Her Majesty's Revenue and Customs (HMRC) the VAT they have paid on their costs and overheads. This is a huge advantage.
- **VAT exempt:** VAT exempt goods and services (like care home fees) are outside the VAT regime and are therefore not liable to tax. If an organisation only provides exempt supplies (like a care home operator) they cannot register for VAT and cannot therefore recover the VAT they have paid on costs incurred by making the exempt supplies. This is a big disadvantage.

There is excellent further information on what rates apply to various goods and services on the government website **www.gov.uk/vat-rates**.

So, which organisations/businesses are obliged to collect VAT?
Businesses which have total sales/income (not profit) above a threshold (which in 2016/17 was £83,000) are legally required to be registered (with a VAT number) with HM Revenues and Customs (HMRC) to collect VAT. Businesses with total income under this threshold can decide whether it is in their interests to be voluntarily registered.

How does a business manage its VAT?
A registered business keeps a note in its accounts of all the VAT it has collected from all its customers. For example this might be £10,000 in three months (a quarter).

In its accounts the business also keeps a note of all the VAT it has paid out for goods and services it needs in order to run its business. This might be £6,000 for the same quarter.

The business then does calculations as to whether it owes money to HMRC or is owed money:

- If the business has collected more VAT money than it has paid out the difference is what it owes HMRC. In the example above subtracting the £6,000 paid out in VAT from the £10,000 collected results in the business owing HMRC £4,000.
- If the business has paid out more in VAT than it collects from its clients the difference is what HMRC owes it. For example if it collects £10,000 VAT but pays out £14,000 VAT it will be owed £4,000 by HMRC (happy days).

Businesses are legally obliged to make quarterly VAT returns to HMRC with their calculations for whether they owe VAT or are owed money:

- **If money is owed to HMRC,** payment has to accompany the VAT return. The challenge for some companies, especially start-ups growing quickly, is that the calculations have to be done on amounts invoiced rather than money actually received in payment and if the invoice recipients (debtors) are slow to pay this can cause serious cashflow problems for them.
- **If money is owed by HMRC** because the businesses have paid more VAT than they have collected, they can make a polite request to HMRC for a refund.

Get advice
VAT can be a notoriously complicated tax to administer (it is sometimes called **V**ery **A**wkward **T**ax) so, should complications arise, it is best – and will probably save you money in the long run - to get specialist advice from an accountant or VAT consultant.

Self-directed reflection
Our advice is not to reflect on VAT unless you absolutely have to!

Mindfulness

"Mindfulness is the ability to pay attention, in the present moment, without judgement" – Jon Kabat Zinn

The many and varied demands on the care home manager can result in scattered attention and feeling overwhelmed, leading to stress and potential burnout. Often the state of mind of the manager is then felt directly by care staff and passed on to residents and family members. Mindfulness brings benefits to care managers and care staff – when mindfulness is learnt and applied throughout a home, a more mindful and compassionate approach to care can be sustained.

Mindfulness is a therapeutic technique designed to achieve a calm mental state. This is done by focusing on the present moment, all the while acknowledging and accepting one's feelings, thoughts, and bodily sensations. It is very much about acceptance, meaning that we value our thoughts and feelings without judging them – without believing, for instance, that there's a 'right' or' 'wrong' way to think or feel at any one moment.

Mindfulness is a simple form of meditation that was hardly known in the West until recently. Many people are still a little wary when they hear the word 'meditation'. So before we move on, it might help to put some facts in front of you:

- Meditation is not a religion. Many people who practise meditation are themselves religious, but then again, many atheists and agnostics are keen meditators too.
- Mindfulness is simply a method of mental training. You don't have to sit cross-legged on the floor (like the pictures you may have seen in magazines or on TV), but you can if you want to. Most people sit on chairs or on the floor on a cushion to meditate, but what is exciting is you can also practise bringing mindful awareness to whatever you are doing, on buses, trains or while walking to work. You can meditate more or less anywhere.
- Mindfulness does not need a lot of time to practice, although some patience and persistence are required. Many people soon find that meditation frees them from time pressures, so they have more to spend on other things they enjoy.
- Meditation is not complicated. Nor is it about 'success' or 'failure'. Even when meditation feels difficult, you will be learning valuable things about the workings of your mind.
- Mindfulness does not deaden your mind, limit your ambition or prevent you from striving towards important career or lifestyle goals. It will not trick you into behaving passively.
- Meditation is not about accepting the unacceptable. It is about seeing the world with greater clarity so that you can take wiser and more 'thought-full' action to change things which need changing.
- Meditation encourages a deep and compassionate awareness that allows you to think about your real goals and find the best path for you to live the life you want.

Mindfulness is about observation without criticism; being compassionate with yourself. When unhappiness or stress threaten, rather than taking it all personally, you learn to treat these emotions as if they were black clouds in the sky, observing them with friendly curiosity as they drift past. In effect, mindfulness allows you to stop negative thought patterns before they cause you to spiral downwards. It begins the process of putting you back in control of your life.

Over time, mindfulness helps to improve mood, levels of happiness and wellbeing. There is research evidence that mindfulness not only prevents depression, but it can also positively influence the brain patterns which underlie day-to-day anxiety, stress, depression and irritability so that when these symptoms start, they can also disappear more easily. Other scientific studies have shown that people who practise mindfulness see their doctors less often and spend fewer days in hospital. Memory appears to improve, creativity increases and reaction times become faster.

The evidence for the benefits of mindfulness is growing rapidly. The benefits include:

- **Increased patience** – in our fast paced instant gratification culture, it is so easy to become distracted. Mindfulness teaches us to practice patience so it comes more easily to us when we need it.
- **Better focus and productivity** – mindfulness helps us to recognise unwanted interruptions and unhelpful thoughts and to remain focused on the task at hand.
- **Increased compassion** – mindfulness helps us to broaden our compassion for ourselves and others by helping us to suspend judgement and to return to the present moment.
- **Heightened body awareness** – we tend to lose awareness of what our body is feeling when we get too busy or distracted. With mindful awareness we can listen to our bodies, and respond in healthier purposeful ways.
- **Reduced stress and anxiety** – by learning to be more conscious of where we place our attention, we can rewire our brains and our thought patterns resulting in increased feelings of calm and connection with others.

Mindfulness resources

- *Finding the Space to Lead: A Practical Guide to Mindfulness.* Bloomsbury. By Janice Marturano, a senior executive with decades of experience in Fortune 500 corporations who lays out her ideas on mindfulness
- *Mindful Nation UK*: report by the Mindfulness All-Party Parliamentary Group (www.themindfulnessinitiative.org.uk/publications/mindful-nation-uk-report)
- *Be Mindful*: a report by the Mental Health Foundation (www.mentalhealth.org.uk/publications/be-mindful-report)
- *The Compassionate Community* – by Andy Bradley with Francis Briers, available from Pavilion Publishing
- *The Art of Mindfulness*: a Harper One Select book. This selection by Thich Nhat Hanh from his bestselling The Art of Power illuminates the core Buddhist concept of mindfulness for the Western reader.
- *The Miracle of Mindfulness*, by Thich Nhat Hanh. In this beautifully written book, Buddhist monk and Nobel Peace Prize nominee Thich Nhat Hanh explains how to acquire the skills of mindfulness.
- *Wherever you go, There you are*, by Jon Kabat Zinn. Abebooks.
- *A Mindfulness Guide for the Frazzled* by Ruby Wax. Penguin. The comedian draws on personal experience to show how to live a happier life.
- Mindful Leadership: Maria Gonzalez. John Wiley & Sons.
- Meditation apps: www.theguardian.com/technology/2016/may/26/five-of-the-best-meditation-apps
- Oxford Mindfulness Centre, Oxford: www.oxfordmindfulness.org
- The Kings Fund, London
- www.artofmindfulness.org.uk
- www.mindfulnet.org
- www.mindfulnessforstudents.co.uk
- www.headspace.com
- www.kingsfund.org.uk
- www.londonmindful.com
- www.getselfhelp.co.uk/mindfulness
- www.frameworks4change.co.uk/
- www.franticworld.com

Mindfulness quotes

- "Mindfulness is simply being aware of what is happening right now without wishing it were different; enjoying the pleasant without holding on when it changes (which it will); being with the unpleasant without fearing it will always be this way (which it won't)." – James Baraz
- "The moment one gives close attention to anything, even a blade of grass, it becomes a mysterious, awesome, indescribably magnificent world in itself." – Henry Miller
- "Your vision will become clear only when you look into your heart. Who looks outside, dreams. Who looks inside, awakens." – Carl Jung
- "You have a treasure within you that is infinitely greater than anything the world can offer." – Eckhart Tolle
- "Drink your tea slowly and reverently, as if it is the axis on which the world earth revolves – slowly, evenly, without rushing toward the future; live the actual moment. Only this moment is life." – Thich Nhat Hanh
- "Mindfulness is about being fully awake in our lives. It is about perceiving the exquisite vividness of each moment. We also gain immediate access to our own powerful inner resources for insight, transformation, and healing." – Jon Kabat-Zinn
- "Mindfulness is the aware, balanced acceptance of the present experience. It isn't more complicated than that. It is opening to or receiving the present moment, pleasant or unpleasant, just as it is, without either clinging to it or rejecting it." – Sylvia Boorstein
- "There are only two ways to live your life. One is as though nothing is a miracle. The other is as though everything is a miracle." – Albert Einstein
- "Keep knocking and the joy inside will eventually open a window and look out to see who's there.'' – Rumi

Glossary of financial and commercial terms

ACA
The Association of Chartered Accountants is the well-respected professional body for accountants.

Accounts
An individual's or company's financial records. Also an arrangement to keep money with a financial institution, eg a bank or building society.

Account payable
The amount due for payment to a supplier of goods or services also described as a **trade creditor**.

Account receivable
An amount due from a customer also described as a **trade debtor**.

Accounting
The process of identifying, measuring and communicating financial information about an organisation, charity or business to permit informed judgements and decisions by users of the information.

Accounting period
Time period for which financial statements are prepared (eg month, quarter, year), normally one year.

Accruals concept
Payment for goods and services are put into the accounts when goods and services are actually delivered not when the payments are made for them.

Administration expenses (or general and administrative costs or overheads)
Costs that are not directly involved in supplying the goods and services provided by one organisation to another. Generally these are fixed and do not vary with production.

AIM
The Alternative Investment Market in London is a stock market for younger, smaller and less-established companies.

Amortisation
Similar concept to depreciation but instead for intangible assets such as patents or goodwill.

Assets
Anything of value owned by an organisation which has economic value and can be measured and expressed in monetary terms. Examples include cash, investments, inventory, supplies, land, buildings, equipment, and vehicles.

Audit
The inspection (usually annual) of an organisation's books and financial statements by auditors.

Auditor
An accountant appointed to carry out an organisation's audit.

Auditor's report
The written opinion of an independent certified public accountant that a company's financial statements are a fair representation of the company's financial performance and financial position. The auditor's report is required for companies traded on stock-markets and as reassurance to help the reader to make decisions based on the results of the audit.

Back office
The team that deals with all the admin and support functions of a business.

Bad debt
Money owed that can no longer be recovered normally due to a debtor going bankrupt.

Balance sheet
One of the main financial statements. The balance sheet reports an organisation's assets and liabilities at a specific point in time, such as on 31 December.

Bond
A bond is a debt investment in which an investor loans money to an organisation (typically a company or government) which borrows the funds for a defined period of time at a variable or fixed interest rate. Bonds are used by companies, municipalities, states and sovereign governments to raise money and finance a variety of projects and activities.

Break-even point
The break-even point is the point at which total income exactly matches total costs so neither a loss or profit is made. It indicates the base level of activity needed from which a profit can be made.

Budget
An estimate of total revenues and costs over a specified period, reflecting a reading of future financial conditions and goals. As one of the most important financial tools, a budget serves also as (1) a plan of action for achieving quantified objectives, (2) a standard for measuring performance, and (3) a device for coping with foreseeable adverse situations.

Business angel
Private individual who invests in new and entrepreneurial businesses with the purpose of making a substantial capital gain and often also contributing expertise to the management.

Burn-rate
The speed at which a start-up uses cash.

Capital
An amount of finance provided to enable a business to acquire assets and sustain its operations.

Capital expenditure
Spending on fixed assets of a business such as property, plant and equipment, shown in the balance sheet.

Cashflow
The total amount of money being transferred into (positive cash-flow) and out of an organisation (negative cash-flow) , especially useful for deciding whether the organisation will have enough money to pay its bills.

Cashflow statement
The financial statement of a business which summarises its total cash inflows and outflows.

Compliance
The department of an organisation which deals with regulatory issues – ensuring the organisation is abiding by the law.

Compound interest
Interest which is not removed from an investment but rather reinvested with the purpose of creating a bigger balance.

Consistency
Definitions, practices and assumptions should be consistent within an organisation, and consistently applied over time so that trend comparisons can be undertaken. Where there are changes, then the financial implications of these need to be communicated and quantified in the formal accounts that are prepared. For example, varying how depreciation is calculated will affect the amount that the P&L shows for the depreciation cost for the period.

Cooking the books
Describes a deceitful accounting scheme deliberately designed to mislead.

Corporation tax
Tax paid by companies (with some notable exceptions) on 'chargeable' profits. Rates are decided by the government and tend to be lower for smaller companies.

Cost accounting
Managerial accounting which calculates, records and controls the operating costs of producing goods or services.

Cost-benefit analysis
Analysis of the costs and benefits of an investment to establish whether the investment is worth doing from a purely accounting point of view.

Cost centre
A **team**, business area or department that only incurs costs.

Cost of Goods Sold (COGS)
These are the direct costs attributable to the production of the goods sold by a company. This amount includes the cost of the materials used in creating the good along with the direct labour costs used to produce the good. Also referred to as 'cost of sales'.

Creditor
A person or business to whom money is owed.

Credit control
An activity carried out by a business to ensure that it gives **credit** only to customers who are able to pay, and that customers pay on time.

Credit crunch
A time when a business is short of cash and finding it difficult to raise loans – especially at reasonable interest rates.

Crowdfunding
A way of funding a project or venture by raising monetary contributions from a large number of people.

Current assets
These assets are expected to be used within a year. They are further categorised into stock (or inventory), debtors and cash, with the latter being assumed to be the most 'liquid' ie readily usable. Note that in some organisations and sectors, particularly manufacturing, stock is further categorised into raw materials, work in progress and finished goods.

Current liabilities
Money owed that needs to be repaid within 12 months.

Debenture
A long-term security yielding a fixed rate of interest, issued by a company and secured against its assets (in the UK). They are the most common form of long-term loans that can be taken by a company.

Debt capital
The capital that a business raises by taking out a loan, normally repayable at a future date.

Debtor
A person or business who owes money to an organisation following the purchase of goods and/or services on credit.

Depreciation
The spreading of the cost of a capital item over an agreed period. For example, a piece of equipment costing £10k having a life of five years might be depreciated over five years.

Dividends
Dividends are a distribution of corporate earnings to company shareholders in direct proportion to the number (and type) of shares they own. They come out of taxed earnings and are usually either cash or shares.

EBIT/EBITDA
Earnings Before Interest and Tax / Earnings Before Interest, Tax, Depreciation and Amortisation. They are both measures of profitability on a profit and loss account or income statement. EBITDA is the best way to compare profitability or surplus between organisations because it offers the fairest comparison between organisations which have been financed differently.

Equity
In accounting terms, **equity (or owner's equity)** is the difference between the value of the assets and the value of the liabilities of something owned, according to the equation:
Equity = Assets - Liabilities

For example, if someone owns a nursing home worth £15m (an asset), but owes £5m to a bank secured against the home (a liability), the owner will have £10m of equity. Equity can be negative if liabilities exceed assets. **Shareholders' equity** (or stockholders' equity, shareholders' funds, shareholders' capital or similar terms) is the equity of a company as divided among its shareholders. Negative shareholders' equity is often referred to as a shareholders' deficit. Finally, equity can refer to the **capital stock of a company**. The value of the stock depends on the company's future economic prospects. For a company in liquidation, the equity is that which remains after all liabilities have been paid.

Estates management
The part of the back office which deals with maintenance and the legal functions of the buildings and land the company occupies or owns.

Expenditure or Expenses
Money paid out by the organisation.

Exit strategy
In financial terms, a plan to end involvement with a business or investment while making the greatest possible profit (or smallest possible loss). An exit strategy is designed to turn an illiquid asset into liquid cash for the investor.

Facilities management
The part of the management team which deals with the admin of the services a company needs eg mailroom, catering, cleaning.

Fixed assets
Fixed assets are assets that are held for use by the business rather than for sale. They are expected to stay within the organisation for an extended period of time (usually more than one year but in practice most will last longer than this). Typical fixed assets would be buildings, land, equipment, vehicles and computer hardware. Major items of software (operating systems and substantial application packages - but not usually routine maintenance) are also included. Also licences where a single payment is made covering the expected life of the software.

Front of house
The part of the management team which interacts with clients in person eg reception, care staff, catering staff serving food.

FTSE ('FOOTSIE') 100
Footsie is the slang term for the Financial Times Actuaries 100 index (FTSE 100), the index which consists of the 100 largest companies that trade on the London Stock Exchange. Globally it is one of the most important indices of share performance. (There is also a FTSE 250 index.)

GDP
Gross Domestic Product measures a country's total annual output in goods and services.

Gearing
The relationship between a company's debt capital and its equity. The higher the level of debt, the more highly geared the company is and the more it is at risk should anything serious go wrong.

Going concern
The going concern principle means accounts are prepared on the basis that the organisation is going to continue to exist and trade for the foreseeable future. Assets are shown at the value they provide to ongoing operations, not at the level they might reach on the open market.

Goodwill
Goodwill has two meanings. It can either mean the excellent product, brand name or reputation which gives a competitive advantage to an organisation. This goodwill does not show on the balance sheet. Or an organisation may pay cash for the goodwill which another business has built up over the years and this does show on the balance sheet.

Gross profit
The figure left over when cost of sales (all expenses) has been deducted from the income (turnover).

H&S
Health and safety. Employers have a duty to ensure health and safety procedures are put in place to prevent staff from being harmed or becoming ill due to work practices.

HR
Human resources – the department that is responsible for all matters that relate to employing staff; includes paying staff, holidays, sickness records, recruitment, appraisal, disciplinary issues and sometimes training and performance.

Insider trading
Illegally buying or selling shares using information not known to the general public.

Intangible assets
Intangible assets are ongoing sources of value to an organisation which are not visible or touchable in the same way as fixed and current assets are. Typical examples include copyrights, intellectual property rights, patents and brands.

IP
Intellectual Property – the company's copyrights, patents and brands.

IPO
Initial Public Offering. The first offer to the general public of a company's shares.

Liability
Something that is owed, an obligation. These are divided broadly into short-term commitments (usually up to 12 months) and long-term ones. In financial terms, liabilities usually describe the money lent to organisations by, say, banks or financial institutions. Liability also describes the extent to which shareholders or partners are personally responsible for the debts of their company. Unlimited liability eg for partnerships means that the partners are required to pay the debts of the business personally and in full. For limited liability (Ltd) see below.

Ltd
Letters which come after a company's name to show that it is a private limited liability company. This is a company whose shareholders have limited their risk/liability to the amount of money they used to pay for their shares. Limited companies may be limited by shares or by guarantee.

Logistics
In company terms, this is the part of the company which deals with getting the company goods and services to the client as quickly and cheaply as possible.

M&A
Mergers and acquisitions. When two separate companies join together they are said to have merged. If one buys out the other then there has been an acquisition.

Overheads
General administrative, manufacturing or sales costs which cannot be linked to a particular product, good, service or revenue source. Examples include the expenses of running a company's HQ, rates, maintenance, IT and catering.

Payroll expenses
The amount of salaries and wages paid to employees in exchange for services rendered by them to a business. The term may also be assumed to include the cost of all related payroll taxes.

PBIT
Profit Before Interest and Tax.

Pension fund trustees
A body which is independent of a company, usually made up of the finance director, employees and external experts, which looks after the company's pension fund.

Petty cash
Company cash used to pay small, everyday expenses which are then carefully recorded for accounts.

PLC
Public Limited Company.

PR
Public relations: An exercise by the company to strategically manage communication between the company and its public so that the company is seen in the best light possible.

Prepayments
A company may pay for goods or services before they have been received. Any amounts that have been paid for goods and services not received by the end of an accounting period are shown in the balance sheet as prepayments. These amounts will not be shown as costs in the P&L.

Profit and Loss (P&L)
One of the three main business reporting and measuring tools. The summarised record of all the sales income (turnover) and costs of an organisation over a stated period of time. A profit is achieved when the income exceeds the costs. A loss is recorded when the costs exceed the sales income.

Profit centre
A team, business area or department that generates revenue and (annoyingly) incurs costs.

Prudence
Financial statements should be prudently or conservatively presented. Losses, for example costs, must be realistically and fairly represented. Also, bad debt risk should be recognised in the accounts as soon as they are identified. Gains should be reflected only when they are definite ie once the customer is invoiced. This is one of the main reasons for 'tensions' between finance and sales teams.

Purchase ledger (UK) or accounts payable (US)
The purchase ledger is a record of a business's purchases and expenses, regardless of whether or not they have been paid and how much is still owed. The purchase ledger has an account for every supplier. This supplier account shows all the transactions for the one supplier including:

- **Purchase invoices**
- **Purchase credit notes**
- **Payments made.**

R&D
Research and development are all the activities undertaken in order to develop a business's services or products.

Retained earnings
The accumulated undistributed earnings of a company retained for future needs or for future distribution to its owners.

Revenue, earnings, or income
Money earned by the organisation.

Revenue expenditure
A revenue expenditure is a cost that is expensed in the accounting year in which it is incurred in the P&L account.

Risk management
The identification of the risks the business is exposed to and then their management to reduce them to the minimum.

Sales ledger (UK) or accounts receivable (US)
Record of those to whom the organisation has sold its goods and services and the amount they owe ie what the organisation expects to receive.

Separability
We need to understand how accounts' figures are made up. If we have sales of £100,001 and costs of £100,000, it would not be sufficient to say we made a profit of £1; we need to know how this was achieved. The accounting rules in any particular country will define how separable the elements within the financial accounts need to be.

Shareholder capital
This figure is made up of the value of shares issued to shareholders and the build-up of retained profit over the lifetime of the organisation. There may also be further reserves and allowances – eg for the revaluation of assets or for bad debts and write offs.

Share options
The granting of rights to employees to buy shares in a company, often at a specific price as an incentive to increase profitability and drive the share price higher.

SMEs
Small and medium-sized enterprises.

Stock
Goods held ready for sale, or raw materials held ready to make into goods, or work in progress. In the US shares are commonly described as stocks.

Turnover
Sales turnover is the company's total revenue, including invoices, cash payments and other revenues during a specified time period – usually a year. Turnover does not include VAT and is reported after any discounts have been applied. The term is often just referred to as sales or net sales, which means revenues without VAT.

Unit cost
The average cost of producing one unit of a good or service, eg a week in a care home. A useful measure to compare costs between providers.

Viability
A business' ability to generate enough income (eg from fees) to meet its operating expenses and financing costs, as well as providing evidence that it has an ongoing future.

Winding up
The process of closing a business by selling all the assets, paying off creditors, making staff redundant and distributing any remaining assets to the partners, shareholders or guarantors.

Index